Study Abroad

Study Abroad
Traditions and New Directions

Edited by
Miriam Fuchs and
Sarita Rai, with
Yves Loiseau

THE MODERN LANGUAGE ASSOCIATION OF AMERICA
New York 2019

Printed in the United States of America

MLA and the MODERN LANGUAGE ASSOCIATION are trademarks owned by the Modern Language Association of America. For information about obtaining permission to reprint material from MLA book publications, send your request by mail (see address below) or e-mail (permissions@mla.org).

Library of Congress Cataloging-in-Publication Data are available from the Library of Congress.

ISBN 978-1-60329-387-7 (cloth)
ISBN 978-1-60329-388-4 (paper)
ISBN 978-1-60329-389-1 (EPUB)
ISBN 978-1-60329-390-7 (Kindle)

Cover illustration of the paperback and electronic editions: Li Shurui, *Polar Lights No. 12*, 2010, acrylic on canvas. Courtesy the artist and private collection.

Published by The Modern Language Association of America
85 Broad Street, suite 500, New York, New York 10004-2434
www.mla.org

CONTENTS

PART THREE | **Offices of Study Abroad and
University Relations**

Introduction: Contexts and Changes in Study Abroad

Miriam Fuchs and Sarita Rai

Contexts

The last thirty years have witnessed steady growth in the number of students participating in study abroad. According to the most recent annual reporting by the Institute of International Education (IIE), the number of university students studying abroad from the United States has more than tripled since the mid-1990s, reaching a high of 325,339 participants in the 2015–16 academic year. Curricula have evolved beyond conventional courses of study in languages and literatures, and destinations have multiplied, enlarging the study abroad landscape beyond traditional sites, such as England, Italy, France, and Spain. Germany and China are respectively the fifth- and sixth-most-popular countries for university students coming from the United States, while Denmark, the Czech Republic, South Africa, and the Netherlands have all showed double-digit growth. Interest in study abroad programs in Cuba, Japan, and South Korea has also increased steadily over the past few years ("IIE Releases"). The institute's data reflect a study abroad landscape that has become more global in scope, more comprehensive in subject matter, and more universal in access and appeal.

Changes

Three recent statistics strike us as nothing short of remarkable. First, most students from American institutions choose to study abroad in short-term programs lasting from ten days to eight weeks ("Duration"). This category is often considered the driving force behind the growth of study abroad, and experts predict that short programs will continue to thrive (Loveland and Murphy; Brubaker). These programs are often more affordable than other alternatives and involve fewer disruptions to family life or employment. They also appeal to student populations that remain underrepresented in longer programs. These include older students, minority students, and students with disabilities, whose numbers in yearlong programs remain relatively low. With 63 percent of study abroad programs for students from the United States now classified as short-term, a host of new formats has replaced the familiar junior year abroad. Some offer travel directed by an individual professor to a region or to multiple sites of relevant academic interest; others are internship, volunteer, or service-learning opportunities; and still others link intensive course work with teacher training, field research abroad, community projects, or partnerships with international institutions. Meanwhile, mid-range programs of one to two quarters or one semester make up 35 percent of the total number, and full academic or calendar year programs have declined steadily to only 3 percent ("Duration"). The long-standing image of an academic or calendar year devoted to intensive language study no longer reflects reality. Administrators and teachers will have to keep apprised of these durational breakdowns and continue to respond with creative and appealing study abroad opportunities.

The second remarkable discovery is that the largest study abroad population from the United States represents the STEM fields of sciences, technology, engineering, and mathematics. Though strict course requirements and the challenges of integrating study abroad programs with STEM curricula tend to discourage enrollment in international programs (Giedt et al. 167), STEM departments now produce a full 25.2 percent of all students from the United States studying abroad, increasing 9 percent between 2014–15 and 2015–16 and pulling ahead of business (20.9 percent) and the social sciences (17.1 percent) ("Fields"). Given these data, it is likely that efforts to gain greater participation by STEM faculty will continue to bear results. As study abroad offices work with technology, science, and mathematics professors, increased curricular integration of major requirements and subjects offered abroad will progress.

The third remarkable discovery is the contraction of study abroad programs of all durations that offer exclusive or intensive language study. The

IIE's 2017 *Open Doors Report on International Educational Exchange* shows that less than 8 percent of study abroad students concentrate on foreign languages ("Fields"). Moreover, foreign language departments and literature faculties are now less likely to control language programs offered abroad. As noted by the Executive Committee of the Association of Departments of Foreign Languages (ADFL), "While in the past programs abroad were under the purview of the language and literature faculties . . . they have now become a centralized enterprise that universities use to provide an international dimension to undergraduate education, as well as to outsource some of their teaching" (72). In fact, "[m]any foreign language departments have lost control over the location, quality, and content of these programs" (72). Foreign language departments on American campuses also face lower overall enrollment, dropping 9.2 percent between 2013 and 2016 and 15.3 percent between 2009 and 2016 (Looney and Lusin). Despite increased enrollment in Korean and Japanese, the lower numbers overall constitute a warning. The ADFL urges department chairs to foster alliances with other institutional stakeholders and to speak up for the role of language study as internationalization, global awareness, and intercultural competencies gain pedagogical emphasis. Pointing to another problem for individual departments, the ADFL supports the right to decline awarding credit if courses given outside the department do not meet departmental standards (73, 74). While both departmental and interdepartmental perspectives are relevant to study abroad, the dynamics between foreign language and institutional elements are hard to deny and will require stepped-up mutual collaboration.

Meanwhile, research on second language acquisition continues to be a substantial resource in the literature on study abroad. The Modern Language Association and the ADFL are active in noting current trends and outlooks. Volumes in the Teaching Languages, Literatures, and Cultures series such as Janet Swaffer and Katherine Arens's *Remapping the Foreign Language Curriculum: An Approach through Multiple Literacies*, Heidi Byrnes's *Learning Foreign and Second Languages: Perspectives in Research and Scholarship*, and Charles J. Stivale's *Modern French Literary Studies in the Classroom: Pedagogical Strategies* look at research and methodologies for gaining language proficiency, and Gayle Zachmann's "Overseas Engagements: The Presence and Futures of Study Abroad," in Stivale's collection, follows the evolution of the language study abroad program at the University of Florida. *Language Learners in Study Abroad Contexts* (Dufon and Churchill) covers specific pragmatic language competencies to abstract concerns such as student motivation and attitudes. And journal essays on language acquisition continue to be a mainstay of the literature with, for example, a cluster of articles in the Fall 2014 issue of *Frontiers: The Interdisciplinary Journal of Study Abroad* (see Liu Li; Jochum; Savage and Hughes).

Yet stakeholders in study abroad must also look to publications in education, administration, pedagogy, linguistics, psychology, and sociology, as well as literature and the humanities. Numerous full-length works, such as *Study Abroad: The Experience of American Undergraduates* (Carlson et al.) and *Student Learning Abroad: What Our Students Are Learning, What They're Not, and What We Can Do About It* (Vande Berg et al.), are situated in the field of education while others, such as Joshua McKeown's *The First Time Effect* and *Assessing Study Abroad: Theory, Tools, and Practice* (Savicki and Brewer), examine measures of assessment, a major factor for many institutions and accrediting agencies. *NAFSA's Guide to Education Abroad for Advisers and Administrators* (Hoffa et al.) studies education abroad within the context of American higher education, various aspects of student advising, and program planning and evaluation. The selections in *The Sage Handbook of International Education* (Deardorff et al.) range from internationalization within historical and conceptual contexts to global trends in education both in the United States and abroad. The two-volume history of study abroad published by *Frontiers: The Interdisciplinary Journal of Study Abroad* (Hoffa; DePaul and Hoffa) offers informative and statistically rich essays that often focus on empirical and evaluative data. *Frontiers* continues to publish analyses of students' intellectual and cognitive development in international and intercultural settings and is a valuable resource for educators navigating a field that is not organized as a single discrete discipline.

The literature on study abroad also encompasses guides and handbooks for students and parents on study abroad providers, institutions, and third-party consortia. These resources come in numerous formats—hard copy, e-books, and sometimes downloadable pdf files. Books such as *The Global Classroom: An Essential Guide to Study Abroad* (Lantis and DuPlaga) and *Prepare for Departure: A Guide to Making the Most of Your Study Abroad Experience* (Story), which are targeted to prospective students, outline preparation, participation, and postprogram processes, and often go beyond the basics to emphasize studying abroad as "a holistic intellectual and emotional journey" (Lantis and DuPlaga ix). Titles such as *The Handbook of Research and*

Practice in Study Abroad: Higher Education and the Quest for Global Citizenship (Lewin) and *Promoting Inclusion in Education Abroad: A Handbook of Research and Practice* (Hamir and Gozik) look at developments in international education while still others focus on individual geographical sites: *Decoding China: A Handbook for Traveling, Studying, and Working in Today's China* (Christensen) and Maria Espinoza's *Study, Abroad in Spain: Everything You Need to Know About Studying in Spain.* Organizations such as the IIE publish guides and short books, for example, *A Student Guide to Study Abroad* and its companion *A Parent Guide to Study Abroad* (Berdan). *IIE Passport 2014–15: The Complete Guide to Study Abroad Programs* provides a multitude of study abroad sites along with information on all aspects of the study abroad experience.

Despite the plethora of resources on study abroad, professors, students, and programs suffer from a lack of communication and collaboration across universities and departments. Access to model programs and tested curricula help instructors develop creative courses that attract students and maintain academic rigor. Yet virtually none of the literature collects in one volume a series of discussions and examples of language instruction, other academic areas, and administration and university relations. We believe, then, that our volume satisfies a particular need by providing teachers, international education specialists, and nonspecialists with examples of courses from representative programs along with their pedagogical and learning emphases and discussions of important programmatic issues.

Our approach draws upon the multidisciplinary range of research on study abroad, investigating reported reasons for wanting to study abroad and the psychology of reentry; predictors of success; predeparture and postreturn components; assessment; methods of measuring intercultural competence skills and oral competencies (Stemler et al.); applications of geocritical theory (Walonen); the impact of studying abroad on developing awareness of global citizenship and long-term career choices; and the benefits of service learning. We have consulted essays on the role of pedagogical variables (Spenader and Retka), longitudinal studies of intercultural development (Rexeisen et al.), the role of wonderment (Engberg and Jourian), and even the impact of a semester abroad on students' religious faith and vocational calling identity (Poag and Sperandio; Miller-Perrin and Thompson).

Celeste Kinginger's 2009 *Language Learning and Study Abroad: A Critical Reading of Research* helped us clarify our project goals, particularly by considering how schools design their study abroad offerings and what students expect from their experience. Kinginger calls for attention to lesser-studied programs that involve, say, Asian students studying in Australia, Latin American students in the United States and Europe, African students in Europe, or student exchanges from the Middle East. We found that under-represented student populations also merit closer attention where data are currently sketchy; for example, there are few statistics on support services for LGBT students studying abroad. Information on students with disabilities, too, is hard to come by. Though the 2015 IIE statistics for 2015–16 show a significant gain from the previous year in students with disabilities who study abroad—from 5.3 percent to 8.8 percent ("Students")—80 percent of higher education institutions in the United States do not track figures for students with disabilities who study abroad, and only "18% of all higher education institutes responded to the Open Doors 2014 requests for disability statistics" (Naturale). NAFSA: Association of International Educators is keenly aware that students with disabilities are increasingly asking about available options overseas and emphasizes that education abroad offices are forming coordinated advising procedures.

One significant opportunity for coordinated service to underrepresented students is the IIE's Generation Study Abroad. Founded in 2014, Generation Study Abroad is a coalition of over 150 institutions across more than forty states, with pledges from other countries and the United States Department of State's Bureau of Educational and Cultural Affairs, businesses, private donors, and educators to double the number of students who study abroad by 2020 ("Institute"). The initiative also seeks to increase diversity in race, gender, ethnicity, socioeconomic status, academic discipline, and destination among participants electing to study abroad. If successful, this endeavor could raise total enrollment in study abroad to well over 600,000 students per year. The project is also an opportunity to sustain and refine, as well as to innovate, all the pedagogical aspects of education that make the study abroad experience worthwhile, academically valuable, and safe. Predeparture seminars, postreturn discussions and presentations, risk management seminars, and on-site support services (abroad and at the home institution) are crucial and must be accessible to all students. These objectives call for deliberate collaborative efforts at shared governance, honoring the priorities and expectations of all stakeholders and balancing efforts to increase student numbers with attention to academic quality and control.

Our collaboration is a case in point. One editor is a professor of English with considerable experience teaching study abroad and an interest in art, literature, and cultural studies. One is a pedagogical director of language studies, specializing in teaching language to foreign students, at a university in France. And another editor, specializing in the impact of globalization, is a director of a study abroad center with nearly thirty programs from South America to India to the Pacific. As faculty members in our respective areas, we naturally have varying perspectives that helped us prepare and evaluate initial proposals and early drafts of contributors' submissions using different expectations. We saw how our perspectives gave our editorship energy and rigor. One of us prioritized the academics and creativity of courses the authors had taught; one looked for measurable data to support the proposed hypotheses; and one sought out essays that conceived of specific policy innovations or institutional study abroad paradigms. We therefore believe that the varied topics and organization of our volume will be useful and will encourage readers to think about essays that they otherwise might not read and gain a sense of study abroad from a collection of viewpoints.

Purpose and Organization

This volume was created as a resource for persons and institutions responsible for teaching and innovating programs abroad. It is designed not only to inform the reader about policies, procedures, and programmatic concerns but also to present a diverse picture of study abroad courses around the globe available to students from the United States. The contributors discuss their experiences in a wide range of locations in Asia, Africa, Europe, the Caribbean, and Central America. They provide analyses for enhanced learning, current dialogues about learning theories, pedagogical descriptions, and visions for the future.

The volume's three sections examine international programs for students from the United States in terms of foreign language acquisition, courses in other disciplines, and administration. Together, the sections implicitly or explicitly address the following questions: How are languages currently being taught in study abroad classes, and what theories of learning and language acquisition dominate? What teaching approaches have resulted from recent language research? What can readers learn from experienced teachers who have created innovative courses in subjects other than second language acquisition? What are the advantages and disadvantages of opening a program in regions outside of the best-known locations? How do some schools blend culture and language courses with science or technology classes? Who is able to initiate service-learning experiences, and how? How are study abroad prototypes being sustained or refigured? What relationships involving faculty members, staff members, students, and administrators make the running of programs abroad possible and dynamic? What does the future look like for study abroad in a world that is becoming less predictable?

Given all these factors, a volume such as this one is necessarily a resource of ideas but not a comprehensive reference. The interdisciplinary and cross-disciplinary nature of the field makes full systematic coverage impossible. The essays we have selected demonstrate contrasting viewpoints and emphases, which we hope will enable readers to assess their own programs and encourage more students to pursue the extraordinary experience of studying abroad.

The Essays

Part 1: The Language-Based Curriculum

Language learning is foundational to study abroad programs. It takes place formally in the classroom and can occur informally in nearly every experience a student has in a host country. This applies generally to all programs whether they are immersion, introductory, or advanced classes; summer, semester, or year durations; consortia-based, service-learning, or interregional or binational partnerships; or internships.

Part 1, which grounds the two sections that follow, opens with Celeste Kinginger's "Overcoming Ethnocentrism in Research on Language Learning Abroad." The essay provides a historical overview of the field and an analysis of the data and theories of second language acquisition. Asking why "some language learners thrive while abroad and others founder," Kinginger finds that studying abroad does not in itself lead to language acquisition. The quality of interaction that leads to optimal learning requires students as well as researchers to overcome their ethnocentric biases. The two selections that follow, describing programs in China and in Italy, are intended as exemplary cases, for the instructors' methodologies are applicable to other classrooms regardless of the language of instruction and host location. Like Kinginger, Li Jin recognizes that being abroad does not spontaneously enhance language learning and that neither proximity nor immersion can guarantee proficiency. Her contribution focuses on sociological and ecological perspectives that are relatively new to the field of second language acquisition, demonstrating how they can enhance the teaching of languages, in her case college-level Mandarin. The third essay, by Tania Convertini, gives an example of a language-immersion program in Rome, run by Dartmouth College, that distinguishes experience from deep learning.

Part 2: Content Courses in English

Because much of the expansion of study abroad has occurred in content courses given in English, Part 2 is the largest of the three sections. Many disciplines encourage students and professors to travel abroad for research, service learning, and international collaboration. Some of these programs require students to enroll in a language class; others do not. Contributors to this section describe their own courses, some traditional and others quite innovative. The range of subject matter, from mathematics to service learning to contemporary popular fiction, is striking, and the essays bear out the observation that study abroad growth rates have gone hand-in-hand with increasing disciplinary offerings.

José Antonio Torralba's essay is a useful guide for administrators and faculty members looking to expand their curriculum with a service-learning component. Service learning, Torralba writes, "dictates a movement away from traditional classrooms and into settings where language or any other skill (math, science, etc.) is the means by which people get things done. In other words, language is not an end in itself." Torralba explains how he arranged for students spending six weeks in Mendoza, Argentina, to work with elementary- and secondary-level instructors in poor urban schools and receive credit for a home campus education course.

Along similar lines, Suniti Sharma and JoAnn Phillion examine over a decade of data on how short-term study abroad experiences influence and develop preservice teachers' awareness of cultural differences between themselves and their students. The authors look at undergraduate education majors whose study abroad in Honduras reshapes the understanding of culture, language, and diversity they will eventually bring to their own classrooms in the United States.

The next two essays illustrate short study tours led by home institution professors. Rosanne Fleszar Denhard's two-week London program is an extension of her course The Arts of Medieval and Renaissance Britain, which she teaches at Massachusetts College of Liberal Arts. Participants pursue "student-generated, faculty-mentored" research projects that culminate in presentations on the MCLA campus and at statewide and regional conferences. Mindi McMann's essay evaluates a three-week study tour to Johannesburg and Cape Town that she cotaught in January 2016. McMann cites the most crucial prerequisite for the success of the study tour: support of the involved departments, the College of New Jersey's Center for Global Engagement, upper-level administrators, and an outside agency providing logistical in-country services.

Monique Chyba's "Expanding the Study Abroad Curriculum: A Case Study in Mathematics" and Miriam Fuchs's "Art (and Lies) in Paris: The Ethics of Popular Literature" form a pedagogical diptych for semesters abroad that use some of the same cultural resources to teach very different disciplines and show the challenges of teaching multinational students in international partnership programs. The courses they devised may well inspire readers to adapt the reading lists, assignments, and learning goals and outcomes to other fields of study nearly anywhere a study abroad program exists.

Part 3: Offices of Study Abroad and University Relations

Chad M. Gasta opens Part 3 with "Best Practices for Planning, Developing, and Sustaining Interdisciplinary Language-Based Study Abroad Programs." As chair of the Department of World Languages and Cultures at Iowa State University (and director of programs in international studies and US Latino/a studies), Gasta founded what is probably "the largest language-based (and language-department-sponsored) study abroad program in the United States." Based in Valencia, Spain, the program offers engineering, business, and biology courses in Spanish and English. Initiating a program of this scope requires good relations with other offices in the university, and Gasta's essay, which he calls a road map for others, is a strong argument for involving individual faculty members in all aspects of planning and working in the program.

Rubén Gallo, who directs the Princeton in Cuba program, describes his university's semester program in Havana, where options for study abroad are rapidly expanding. Gallo covers subjects of immediate concern to readers planning programs in Cuba: academics, living arrangements, research, logistics, and his own curricula for Cuban Literature after the Revolution and for Havana: Urban Anthropology, which he taught while serving as the program's resident director and main liaison.

The third essay in this section, by Sarita Rai, synthesizes a variety of studies in order to suggest forces that will shape study abroad concerns in years to come. "Emerging Issues in Study Abroad" focuses on broadening access to programs, on the relation between exchange and study abroad programs, on globalization and financialization, on study abroad's locus in the structural hierarchy, and on the growing need for safety and security measures.

As the essays show, there really is no limit to the creative and imaginative ways that courses can be adapted for global programs and locations. Our contributors show a commitment to offering students viable and increasingly vital international learning opportunities. In shifting the boundaries of the physical classroom, technologically as well as geographically and demographically, they see the future of education as expansive in its offerings and diverse in its participants. We expect that their views, discussions, and course examples will inspire readers to develop programs that continue to challenge their students and provide meaningful twenty-first-century experiences and education.

PART ONE | *The Language-Based Curriculum*

Overcoming Ethnocentrism in Research on Language Learning Abroad

Celeste Kinginger

As a twenty-year-old marketing major at Mid State University, Beatrice joined a semester-long study abroad program in Paris during the spring semester of 2003 (Kinginger, "Language Learning").[1] Beatrice was among the high-achieving language learners in her cohort, with eight years of previous language study and a presojourn score on the Test de Français International placing her in the Basic Working Proficiency range. Her primary stated rationale for study in Paris was enhancement of her language proficiency. For her obligatory homestay, she was placed with a family whose two daughters, aged seventeen and nineteen, lived at home. The family routinely included Beatrice in their convivial mealtime conversations. In principle everything was in place for a successful homestay involving numerous opportunities to observe everyday cultural practices and for engagement in multigenerational, informal talk.

However, soon after her arrival, Beatrice began to find fault with her experience. Her attempts to make contact with francophone age-peer students through the business school where she was enrolled were entirely unsuccessful. Her Franco-Tunisian hosts lived in a diverse, multicultural neighborhood that Beatrice perceived as a "ghetto." Her hosts' questions about her support for the Bush administration's foreign policy, particularly the invasion of Iraq, put her on the defensive. During this season of heightened hostility toward France in the American media, Beatrice framed her hosts' curiosity as anti-Americanism and absence of respect for her country's role in the Second World War. Beatrice's host sisters invited her to share their social connections, asking her to join a party, but, as she related in a mid-semester interview, Beatrice found the event disappointing: "I'm like, what the hell is this? This is not a party. . . . They all sit there together in this smoke-filled room and talk about, like, . . . intellectual things, and I'm like, this is a party? What are we doing?"

I was primarily interested in the conditions of Beatrice's sojourn that would or would not promote language learning. As an experienced language acquisition researcher, having studied abroad in Paris myself and having worked with learners of French for several decades, I contextualized the findings to the best of my ability, drawing support from sociocultural and historical theory (Lantolf and Thorne) and particularly from the notion of collective remembering, or the ideological backdrop of prior texts through which my participants interpreted the phenomena they encountered (Wertsch). Yet, in keeping with standard practice, my report on Beatrice's experience relied chiefly on data from Beatrice: test scores, interviews, and logbook and journal entries. I had no contact with Beatrice's hosts, teachers, or program administrators and never asked for their opinion.

Had I taken the trouble to include the voices of my participants' French hosts, it might have become clearer that Beatrice's numerous complaints corresponded to ethnographic "rich points" (Agar 100): loci of conflict presenting occasions for learning about culture and language use. Had my study included a parallel design, with French participants studying in the United States, real insights about these rich points might have emerged. I might have discovered, for example, that French students are just as dismayed by American practices as was Beatrice when encountering a typical party in France. In documenting the perspectives of French students in Australia, Marie-Claire Patron found that early in their sojourn these students were deeply shocked by the notion of "bring your own bottle" festivities, by excessive consumption of alcohol, and by the absence of companionable discussion of "intellectual things."

Research on Language Learning in Study Abroad

This project and similar qualitative or hybrid studies nevertheless represent an expansion of the scope of American scholarly inquiry into the role of context in language learning abroad. In the latter decades of the twentieth century, research on language education and second language acquisition was strongly influenced by utilitarian models of language and computational models of the mind. In brief, our utilitarian understanding of language accompanied the rise of the proficiency movement, in which the practical applicability of language learning was to take precedence over understanding of language and culture. Having become disassociated from the Modern Language Association through the 1966 establishment of a separate professional organization (the American Council on the Teaching of Foreign Languages), the foreign language teaching profession in the 1980s embraced proficiency as the hallmark of its new relevance. Equipped with a standard measure of speaking ability (the Oral Proficiency Interview, or OPI), the profession would concentrate on fostering the development of useful abilities to interact in foreign languages. The prevailing understanding of the mind and of learning was strongly influenced by computational metaphors, upheld by popularized versions of second language acquisition research, many of which were informed by Noam Chomsky's view of language learning as a universal human biological capacity. Context of learning, in this view, is of little relevance except to the extent that the context provides input suited to the processing capacities of the mind's computational architecture.

In this environment, research on language learning abroad naturally focused on two concerns: first, what learners can do with language after they have studied abroad, and, second, whether or not the study abroad context is in fact an input-rich environment for learning. As I've summarized elsewhere, the story of the research on postsojourn language competence shows an ever-increasing particularity of focus (*Language Learning*). The earliest research relied on holistic constructs, especially proficiency and fluency. Then, when the OPI proved too blunt an instrument to measure gains, especially at the upper levels, researchers began to examine components of communicative ability, including grammatical, lexical, discursive, strategic, or sociolinguistic competence. Much of this research took a fairly simplistic approach to the definition of second-language ability as approximation of native or native-like norms. For example, the literature includes numerous studies of speech acts, such as apologies, compliments, or refusals, in which the performance of study abroad veterans is compared with a native speaker database and usually deemed deficient in various ways. Overall, the research on linguistic outcomes shows that study abroad is a useful, if imperfect, environment for language learning. Yet the one near constant in the findings of this research is inconsistency. That is, the majority of studies find significant individual differences in outcomes, to the point where one researcher suggested that study abroad amplifies the variation in gains to be had from classroom instruction (Huebner, "Effects").

In order to understand why some language learners thrive while abroad and others founder, researchers sought to assess the extent to which study abroad really does offer access to input. Findings on individual differences launched a quest to correlate quantifications of students' reported experiences with measures of language ability. Sometimes this procedure yielded interpretable results; sometimes it did not. Barbara Freed and colleagues, for example, examined measures of fluency in French in the light of data from Language Contact Profile questionnaires for students at home, in study abroad, and in an intensive domestic immersion program. Their findings indicate that time spent engaged in French-mediated activities does predict fluency gains, with study abroad in second place after domestic immersion and before classroom study. In contrast, Ralph Ginsburg and Laura Miller were astonished to find that no correlation could be established between OPI results and their participants' careful recording, in calendar diaries, of time spent in a range of communicative activities while abroad in Russia. Efforts to document the way students use their time abroad continue and are currently focused on the social networks that participants establish (Mitchell et al.), including the extent to which these networks involve local people. Nonetheless, however specific these measures may become, ultimately they cannot explain why such dramatic individual differences emerge from most studies of outcomes.

These outcomes, in fact, depend on the quality of students' interactions with the people they meet while they are abroad and not just on the amount of contact with native speakers that they enjoy. As qualitative inquiry gradually achieved legitimacy in the field of applied linguistics, researchers began to design holistic or ethnographic projects to study the nature of students' experiences abroad. As I've outlined in *Language Learning and Study Abroad*, the picture emerging from this research shows that, for many American students, active engagement in local activity relevant to language learning is compromised by a variety of institutional and social forces. Some programs choose to downplay local interaction and learning in favor of a model in which a sojourn abroad serves primarily to foster students' maturation toward a worldly adulthood of middlebrow consumerism and infotainment (see Doerr). Meanwhile, the forces of globalization have transformed the communicative environment of sojourners abroad. Increasingly, anglophone students encounter a version of their own language, English as a Lingua Franca (ELF), both in and out of the classroom. However, as native speakers of English who do not necessarily master ELF, they often become unpreferred conversation partners because they fail to accommodate their interlocutors. In an era when many young people find identity and community in online social networks, language learners must actively choose to develop local social networks. Given the relative ease of travel, it has also become commonplace for students to host their parents, friends, and intimate partners while they are abroad, leaving little time to nurture local relationships.

Perhaps more insidious are the ideological forces intervening in students' conceptualizations of their experiences abroad. On the one hand, according to a study of contemporary policy discourses by Joan Gore, study abroad itself is linked in historical continuity with the British grand tour tradition in which young men of elite status were sent to the Continent to achieve sophistication and to collect tales of adventure and works of art before settling into their adult lives. Today, study abroad is a decidedly feminized pursuit and is "perceived as attracting wealthy women to academically weak European programs established in a frivolous Grand Tour tradition" (24). Underlying the view that study abroad programs are fundamentally ineffectual is a prejudicial attitude, reinforced by poor understanding of academic institutions abroad, that education of true quality is only to be found in the United States. Although there are, of course, some students whose motives are shaped by humanist and even humanitarian goals, in the dominant discourses identified by Gore, study abroad is a decorative frill on the educations of elite women. On the other hand, as Block has pointed out, when faced with conflict, American students like Beatrice exhibit a marked tendency to recoil into discourses of national superiority, thus cementing ethnocentric attitudes and limiting occasions for learning.

We might expect to find a corrective to these tendencies in the qualitative research. Yet an unfortunate tendency in this research is to privilege the students' point of view, the perspective of newly arrived, novice interactants who do not necessarily comprehend or appreciate the ways in which their interlocutors understand the phenomena under consideration using their own culturally and historically derived interpretive tools. To take just one example beyond my own earlier study, Valerie Pellegrino-Aveni performed an analysis, based on grounded theory methodology, of themes emerging from the journals of American students in Russia. Her purpose was to examine which factors influence students' decisions to speak out or to withdraw from speaking in the context of second-language "self construction" (7). While the author provides a compelling portrait of the struggles facing language learners abroad, her commitment to an emic portrayal of student experiences means that all features of the environment that were not noticed or recorded in the diaries are excluded from analysis. For instance, the study participants reported instances of bad caretaking on the part of their instructors, who openly criticized them in class. One student, Rebeccah, received a teacher's direct criticism as intentionally hurtful and subsequently abandoned the course. Yet the students' appraisal of the situation was likely shaped by the norms of classroom interaction in the United States, where overt criticism is rigorously avoided and privacy laws forbid public exposure of facts about student performance, while the tone of interaction in the Russian classrooms was likely guided by an understanding of the public and private dimensions of social life that is fundamentally different from the corresponding American tradition (Pavlenko).

Thus far we have seen that second language acquisition research tends to view the inhabitants of distant lands solely as providers of input and support to American students as they develop their language proficiency. In Beatrice's words, "I'm really hoping that my family is receptive to *me* . . . but at the same time will correct *me* in a polite manner. . . . [M]y biggest fear is to go with a family who doesn't correct *me* and to just have to go off what they say and never really know if I'm wrong, or ya know if I messed up or if I said it correctly" (Kinginger, "Language Learning" 69; emphasis added). It is as if the host has no other purpose than to accommodate and instruct American guests in their role as language learners. When studies examining the linguistic outcomes of study abroad revealed significant individual differences in these outcomes, qualitative research offered relevant insights into the various social and ideological forces that may limit students' engagement with the local people they encounter while abroad. Yet, in focusing on students to the exclusion of their hosts, this research is at risk of displaying an ethnocentric bias in which we learn only what is wrong with the rest of the world. In this process, the researchers' own culturally derived interpretive tools are also rendered obscure.

Collaborative Research on Language Socialization

From the above brief overview of the research on language learning in study abroad, two implications emerge. First is the need to study language learning not only as the accumulation of usable, native-like forms but also as a process of acculturation in which forms and meaning exist in dialectic unity. This involves acknowledging "the poststructuralist realization that learning is a non-linear, relational human activity, co-constructed between humans and their environment, contingent upon their position in space and history, and a site of struggle for the control of power and memory" (Kramsch 5). Second is the need for truly ethnographic work taking into account the perspectives of all parties and the qualities of the dialogues they establish.

In my own recent research, the natural choice of framework for meeting these requirements is the study of contextualized language practices through the lens of Vygotskian sociocultural theory (SCT) (Lantolf and Thorne). In brief, SCT is a theory of mind prioritizing the role of language and other forms of semiosis in the higher forms of cognitive development and activity. The theory posits that the biological and the social exist in dialectic unity and that human action, including thinking and speaking, is mediated by psychological tools analogous to physical tools (Kozulin). Through engagement with other human beings and artifacts, humans gradually internalize repertoires for thinking and speaking that are provided by, and dependent upon, the historically evolved environments they frequent (Lantolf and Thorne). Communicative interaction is both the source and the result of internalization; therefore language learning cannot be conceptualized as a process separate from language use. More important, as James Lantolf argues in "Sociocultural Theory: A Dialogic Approach to L2 Research," development depends crucially on both the quality and the quantity of social interaction that is attuned to the learner's potential ability.

Thus, in contrast to research attempting to quantify social network formation, access to input, or time on task, we focus on the evolving qualities of interactions in which student guests and hosts become engaged. We are especially interested in the extent to which these interactions are attuned to the needs of individuals, whether guests or hosts, in the role of learner—that is, the extent to which participants collectively enact Zones of Proximal Development, famously defined as "the distance between the actual developmental level as determined by independent problem solving and the level of potential development as determined through problem solving under adult guidance or in collaboration with more capable peers" (Vygotsky 86).

Our current project examines the microgenetic evolution of the homestay as a learning environment for Chinese host families and the American high school students living with them during a short-term stay in Beijing or

Chengdu. The project is collaborative by explicit design, and, beyond myself, involves a team of Chinese researchers: a highly experienced teacher of Chinese and the director of the study abroad program in question, as well as two advanced doctoral students. During their three-week summer homestays, the eleven student participants were asked to make at least two audio recordings per week of events they found useful for language learning, most often mealtime conversations. The students, as well as their host parents and siblings, were interviewed at the conclusion of the program.

We designed this project to explore the specific interactive practices that had inspired earlier program participants to describe the homestay as a welcoming environment where their language proficiency and cultural awareness increased exponentially (Tan and Kinginger). Three recently published case studies (Kinginger et al., "Short-Term Homestay") illustrate the variety of experience unfolding in these settings, demonstrating that initial proficiency is not the only predictor of a happy and successful homestay. The data involving Sam, a student of advanced proficiency whose interactions are illustrated below, portray the homestay as a context for learning on the part of all concerned, including the host family. Henry, who arrived with proficiency estimated at Intermediate Low, interacted in Chinese with his hosts very infrequently. Perhaps the most interesting case is that of David, who presented estimated initial proficiency lower than Henry's (Novice High) yet showed remarkable development in his ability to interact with his hosts in Chinese. We noted the frequency with which David's family, the Zhaos, engaged in the display of relational identities through situational humor, especially lighthearted teasing. Because teasing normally takes place upon a foundation of shared knowledge about social norms and cultural practices, it is both an index of intimacy and an important aspect of language socialization. David first witnessed his host sister being teased publicly about her school performance in a reflection of family anxiety about college entrance examinations. He was then teased about his food preferences, which ran counter to Chinese views on the importance of a balanced diet. Eventually, in the course of only three weeks and despite his lower proficiency, David became an active contributor to his host family's everyday practice of situational humor.

In our work on contextualized language practices surrounding food and taste (Kinginger et al., "Contextualized Language Practices") we have observed that the participants engaged in several practices highly conducive to learning. Most obviously, host family members explicitly oriented students to the dishes served, naming ingredients and encouraging students to name the foods themselves. In Excerpt 1, for example, Sam (S) requested the name of a particular vegetable and was guided by his host father (HF) in learning to pronounce the corresponding word:

EXCERPT 1

1. S:　*unh*
   zhè zhōngwén jiào shénme
   this Chinese　　call　what
   what is this called in Chinese?

2. HF:　**cài**
   vegetable
   vegetable

3. S:　[zhè shi]
   this　COP
   this　is

4. HF:　[biǎn suān]
   green sour
   green sour
   biǎndòu
   Chinese:green:bean
   Chinese green beans
   zhèi jiùshì　biǎndòu
   this precisely:COP Chinese:green:bean
   to be precise, Chinese green beans

   S:　**biǎndou**
   Chinese:green:bean
   Chinese green beans

   HF:　zhèi jiùshì　biǎndòu
   this precisely:COP Chinese:green:bean
   specifically, these are Chinese green beans

In interactions on the theme of taste ("Short-Term Homestay"), the American guests were exposed in various ways to Chinese culinary aesthetics involving efforts to achieve harmony (*he*) through the skillful mixing and presentation of a variety of foods, with an emphasis on a seasonally appropriate balance of "hot" and "cold" foods (Liu). Henry's host mother, for example, rather sternly insisted that he try cold mung bean soup, although he found it "weird" (18) in part because she believed its cooling properties would contribute to his comfort during the hot Beijing summer. Larry was offered specific lessons on the health benefits of certain foods, such as the reputation of asparagus for preventing cancer. Sam was engaged in a series of debates with his host family, especially with his host mother, who had visited the United States, about the poor quality of American food. When confronted with his host father's claim that the preparation of American spaghetti sauce involves no effort, Sam contested this view. His host mother (HM) complained bitterly about the hamburgers and sandwiches she had been obliged to consume at American fast-food restaurants, so Sam, assisted by his host brother (HB), attempted to come to the defense of the hamburger:

EXCERPT 2

1. S: **unh wǒ wǒ yào gěi ni shuō**
          INT I   I   want give you say
          unh I-I want to give say to you
          nǐ *uh uh*
          you INT INT
          you *uh uh*
          mēi zài mēiguō suóyǒu de hànbǎo bú shì
          Amer in America all   ASSOC hamburgers NEG COP
          In Ameri in America all hamburgers aren't
          bú shì duì shēntǐ bù   hǎo
          NEG COP for body   NEG good
          aren't bad for the body

2. HM: [**èn**]
          INT
          mhm

3. S: [**yīnwei**] **zài méiguó   zhí zhí yǒu *uh***
          because in America   only only exist
          because in America there's only only *uh*
          màidānglāo de   hànbǎo
          McDonald's ASSOC hamburger
          hamburgers from the McDonald's
          tā jiù   shì   bù

> it ADV COP NEG
>
> it's just is not
>
> **duì shēntǐ bù hǎo kěshì**
>
> for body NEG good but
>
> not good for the body but
>
> *unh most* **zhōngwén zěnme shuō**
>
> INT   Chinese   how   say
>
> *unh most* how to say *most* in Chinese?

4. HB: **dàbùfen**

> most
>
> most

5. S: **dàbùfēn dē hànbǎo   shì wǒ**

> most ASSOC hamburger COP I
>
> most hamburger are I
>
> **bú duì shēntǐ bù   hǎo**
>
> NEG for body   NEG good
>
> not bad for the body

6. HM: **dànshì chī hànbǎo**

> but   eat hamburger
>
> but eating hamburgers
>
> **cài   tài shǎo le**
>
> vegetable too few   CRS
>
> too few vegetables

7. S: *uhuh*

8. HM: **ròu**

> meat
>
> meat
>
> **tā lǐmiàn jiùshì**
>
> it inside only:COP
>
> inside it there are only
>
> **liǎng piàn miànbāo**
>
> two CLF bread
>
> two pieces of bread
>
> **zhōngjiān jiā le   yīdiǎnr cài**
>
> middle   add PFV few   vegetable
>
> add few vegetables in the middle
>
> **jiā le liǎng céng ròu**

add PFV two layer meat
add two layers of meat

9. S: *uhuh*

10. HM: cài   tài shǎo le
            vegetable too few   CRS
            too few vegetables
            wǒmen jiù   xíguàn chī
            we   simply used:to eat
            we are simply used to eating
            ēn   bǐjiào duō de cài
            INT relatively many NOM vegetable
            unh relatively more vegetables
            měi yí   dùn fàn ròu chī de shǎo
            every one CLF meal meat eat CSC little
            every meal (we) eat little meat
            dànshì cài   yào   chī de duō
            but vegetable want eat   CSC many
            but want to eat a lot of vegetables

In turns 1–5, including a lexical search assisted by his host brother, Sam nominated the topic of the healthful hamburger. In an attempt very like his earlier defense of pasta sauce, he tried to convince his host mother that her view of the hamburger was an overgeneralization and that a variety of hamburgers exists. Her response in the remaining turns was to observe that hamburgers do not contain enough vegetables and to explain to Sam the Chinese preference for a smaller amount of meat and more vegetables in each meal. Although Sam did not prevail in this instance, he did enjoy an opportunity to explore a controversial topic in a safe environment.

Implications for Research

The level of microethnographic detail in our work on language socialization in Chinese homestays allows us to consider both student and host perspectives. A collaborative approach to interpretation, involving researchers deeply familiar with the cultural practices observed by all participants, lends a comparative perspective, helping us avoid one-sided readings of our data. When the details of socializing interactions are interpreted in relation to the societal and moral values they convey, significant insights about study abroad as a learning environment can emerge. There are of course many limitations involved in our research, including our decision to minimize disruption by recording on the audio channel only, the small number of participants, and our inability to generalize. Studies of this kind must be seen as complementing larger-scale projects enrolling larger numbers of participants in research focusing on specific outcomes such as proficiency, fluency, or specific aspects of communicative ability. However, given an environment where scholarship historically risks perpetuating ethnocentric attitudes, we believe that any research approach honoring native speakers as people is worthy of consideration.

Implications for Language Pedagogy

The evidence makes clear that the professional folklore interpreting study abroad as a context where all students are engaged in high-quality, authentic interactions is only partially grounded in reality. When students truly desire language competence and go abroad in pursuit of a multilingual future, they may require assistance both in negotiating access to learning opportunities and in interpreting the intentions of their hosts.

As students prepare for a sojourn abroad, educators can help them choose programs foregrounding language learning and develop their understanding of the social interactive aspects of language, such as sociolinguistic and pragmatic abilities, best learned outside the classroom. Through computer-mediated communication, students can practice informal interaction with peers and begin to regard native speakers as people rather than merely as providers of linguistic input. Prior training in ethnographic techniques of observation, participation, and reflection has been shown to enhance students' experiences abroad (e.g., Jackson), helping them to navigate rich points and seek local understandings of the phenomena they encounter.

Educators may also play a role in enhancing the quality of students' engagement in their host communities while they are abroad through various tasks, projects, or assignments. Structured conversations with host families or student peers can increase both the quality and the quantity of the dialogic interaction students enjoy. Language-related projects can encourage focused observation (for example, of the linguistic landscape or the language of service encounters), followed by discussions with hosts around culturally unique artifacts. Service-learning arrangements and internships are also valuable, since they can expand both students' range of interactive contexts and their access to local social networks involving people of diverse age and social history.

To help students overcome ethnocentric bias, and thereby take full advantage of study abroad as a context for language learning, researchers must do the same. One proposal is to adopt collaborative and dialogic approaches to scholarship in international education, modeling the same willingness to learn from host communities that we hope to instill in our students.

NOTES

Research for this essay was funded in part by a grant from the Confucius Institute and in part by a United States Department of Education Grant (CFDA 84.229, P229A060003–08) to the Pennsylvania State University. However, the arguments presented here do not necessarily represent the policy of the Department of Education or indicate endorsement by the federal government.

1. This essay reproduces pseudonyms assigned to institutions, host families, and students in the reports cited.

College-Level Mandarin Chinese Study Abroad Pedagogy from an Ecological and Sociocultural Perspective

Li Jin

There is consistent interest among American students in studying abroad in order to increase their foreign language proficiency ("Fields"). However, research continues to demonstrate that learning opportunities such as language interactions and access to resources in study abroad contexts vary drastically for individual learners. Helping learners optimally use resources abroad to develop language proficiency remains a challenge for study abroad administrators and educators. An ecological and sociocultural perspective on second language acquisition (SLA) has been shown to foster communicative competence in meaningful social activities abroad. Demonstrated in the context of a college-level Mandarin Chinese program, this theoretical framework can also inform curricula in other languages and cultures.

An Ecological and Sociocultural Perspective on Language Learning in Study Abroad Contexts

The ecological and sociocultural perspective on language learning is relatively new in SLA. The sociocultural theory (SCT) was introduced into the field of SLA by neo-Vygotskian researchers in the mid-1990s (Lantolf and Thorne 2) and has been widely adopted by researchers and language educators only in the past decade. Other researchers have further expanded this perspective by introducing ecological concepts (Van Lier 3). Language, according to this school of thought, is not a neatly packaged system that can be transmitted from one person to another. Instead, it is a communicative activity in which the users of language dynamically construe meanings when using available linguistic forms in social interaction (Lantolf and Thorne 6). As opposed to more traditional SLA views and theories, such as behaviorism and cognitive interactionism, this perspective views language learning as a meaning-making activity that involves perception, action, interaction, relation, and environment (Van Lier 20). Through highly contextualized and symbolically mediated communication, learners actively appropriate meanings embedded in linguistic forms and cocreate structures of effective language functioning. William Dunn and James Lantolf further assert that "accents, (un)grammaticality, and pragmatic and lexical failures are not just flaws or signs of imperfect learning but ways in which learners attempt to establish (new) identities and gain self-regulation through linguistic means" (427). Besides the innovative view of language and language learning, the ecological and sociocultural perspective on SLA provides two important concepts that are particularly useful to guide the curriculum and course design of study abroad programs: affordances and the zone of proximal development.

Affordances

Leo van Lier introduced the ecological term *affordance* into the field of SLA to replace the traditional term *input*. Affordance is defined as "what is available to the person to do something with" (91) and "the result of perceiving an object while co-perceiving oneself" (105). In contrast to input, which merely identifies available resources, affordance emphasizes the learner's engagement in both perception and action, which varies depending on the learner's awareness and consciousness. Second-language learning occurs only when the resources accessible within the learning environment resonate with learners' capacities, such as their abilities, aptitudes, and attitudes. Van Lier stresses that a learning environment should provide multiple opportunities for learners to deploy all levels of affordances in diverse activities. For instance, subconscious perception enables learners to directly experience a language's prosodic features. By contrast, exercises that require conscious use of language, such as role play and linguistic analysis, help learners develop an in-depth understanding of, and ability to use, the linguistic forms and functions. Fostering multilevel affordances for language learning in a study abroad program should be the focus of curriculum design.

Zone of Proximal Development (ZPD)

From a sociocultural view, learning originates in social interaction and optimally takes place in the zone of proximal development (ZPD), defined as the area between the learner's current and potential proficiency levels (Lantolf and Thorne 263). Potential level is defined as a learner's performance with assistance from a person at a more advanced level. The assistance should be contingent and dynamic according to the learner's needs. Particularly, the learner is considered an active rather than passive assistance receiver, who participates in cooperative problem solving and eventually gains the competence to independently solve the problem. Different from the concepts of feedback and social interaction in other theoretical perspectives, the concept of ZPD stresses appropriate quantity and quality of assistance according to the learner's individual needs as well as the learner's active engagement in the process. Contingent assistance within each learner's ZPD is particularly relevant in optimizing teacher-student and tutor-student interaction in a study abroad program.

The concepts of affordances and the ZPD hold significant potential for transforming Mandarin Chinese pedagogy. The dominant paradigms in the field, especially in China, have been audiolingualism and cognitivism (Wang and Ruan), which foreground rote memorization and teacher-centered instruction. These approaches do little to build the oral communicative skills needed in meaningful social activities. The ecological and sociocultural perspective presents an opportunity to foster linguistic and cultural competence through a more practical and learner-centered pedagogical paradigm.

Chinese Study Abroad Curriculum and Pedagogy Design from an Ecological and Sociocultural Perspective

Design of Program Objectives

It is widely acknowledged that various ostensible and subtle linguistic, social, and cultural cues fail to translate between Chinese and English-speaking

Western cultures. Specifically, Chinese people usually follow distinct inter-actional patterns when conversing with an acquaintance, compared to in-teraction with an outsider. Drawing on a sociocultural perspective, Celeste Kinginger stresses that study abroad students need to be mindful of their identity as peripheral participants in the target culture, and of the impact this identity has on their experience in the target culture ("Enhancing" 68). Failure to understand this or the underlying philosophy embedded in Chi-nese social interaction will hinder attempts to "pick up" Mandarin Chinese in naturalistic settings and to develop socially acceptable language behav-iors (Jin 231). This is true even for advanced-level learners. For instance, the complimenting speech act serves different functions in Chinese and American cultures. The compliments Chinese people give to other Chinese people usually differ from those offered to foreigners. Without a deeper understanding of the rules and values underneath Chinese complimenting, American learners of Mandarin Chinese may face a long and fruitless effort to master this speech act. Therefore, study abroad programs should aim to develop not only linguistic skills but also a deeper understanding of the sociocultural underpinnings behind language behaviors in intracultural and intercultural communication. Only with these goals in place can stu-dents develop the ability to participate effectively in social activities.

Programs aiming to optimize language learning and to help learners gain self-regulation and reconfigure their identities in a foreign culture re-quire thoughtful and rigorous curriculum and pedagogy design. Guided by the ecological and sociocultural perspective, an innovative model of college-level Mandarin Chinese study abroad programs consists of two sets of courses. At each level of proficiency, students take a predeparture culture course to prepare them for their study abroad experience, followed by a se-quence of formal, classroom-based language courses at the study abroad site. The Chinese culture course aims to amplify students' general understand-ing of Chinese culture and society through analyzing language-related prac-tices. The language courses focus on building the Chinese linguistic skills that will enable students to participate in social activities while studying abroad. The two sets of courses should complement each other and jointly help students gain a more profound understanding of Chinese-language ac-tivities and develop the skill set needed for effective participation.

Specifically, the culture course is designed to help students understand historical, social, and cultural facts about Chinese society; the philosophical underpinnings that shape Chinese language use; and the meaning of being an English-speaking learner of Chinese in China.

Language courses are designed to help students develop the vocabulary and sentence patterns needed in various communicative contexts, the oral ability to participate in meaningful communicative activities, and reading and writing skills for various communicative purposes.

Design of Learning Tasks and Materials

The culture course aligns three tasks with its objectives: analysis of a Chinese social practice, maintenance of a weekly reflective journal, and completion of a research project drawn from interviews with Chinese speakers. The three tasks are sequenced according to students' language proficiency level and understanding of Chinese society. The first task is completed before students arrive at the study abroad site; the second task is completed during the study abroad program; and the third task spans the study abroad program but may be completed after students return to their home countries.

Students conduct their social-practice analysis by identifying the values and beliefs embedded in social practices observed in a Chinese film, then comparing Chinese culture with their native culture. They keep journals, in Chinese or in their native language, to enhance their self-awareness of their language growth in China, reflecting on the rich learning points they experience each week and on the methods they are finding effective for learning Chinese language and culture. The research project offers a unique opportunity for students to conduct an in-depth investigation of one Chinese speech act. It is designed to foster a deeper understanding of how sociocultural factors, philosophical underpinnings, and speakers' identities may shape Chinese-language use. By surveying or interviewing both native speakers of Chinese and Chinese-speaking internationals in China, students investigate how one language function, such as greeting or complimenting, is conducted in China, and analyze what social, cultural, or historical factors may influence the language behavior. Students are expected to conduct their research while studying abroad in China but may analyze the data and write their reports after they return home, taking time to thoughtfully interpret the research findings.

The tasks in the language courses are more versatile than those in the culture courses. To foster multilevel affordances, a variety of tasks should be designed to accommodate and relate to students' abilities and attitudes. A preprogram test can identify each individual's language level, preferred language-learning styles, and preferred extracurricular activities. Assigned tasks should take advantage of both structured classroom instruction and the rich authentic language resources offered in a study abroad program, setting expectations and offering assistance as appropriate to each student's level of proficiency.

Most classroom-based activities in foreign language instruction can be adapted for study abroad programs. For instance, students can conduct role-play games with peers, carry out interactive reading exercises, or give oral and written presentations. Outside the classroom, both simple communications and complex projects can help students engage in authentic and meaningful social activities in the immersion environment. Pairing each student with a native Chinese tutor creates daily opportunities for basic, one-on-one interactions, including casual conversations and formal interviews on assigned topics. Meetings may take place on or off campus to incorporate more diverse social settings such as a library, a salon, or a museum. More complex projects expose students to larger-scale social activities that involve a greater number of native speakers of Chinese with more diverse social identities. Each project requires students to participate in an authentic social activity and to document their language-use experience during the activity. For example, students may visit a family at home or attend a seminar organized by the host institution. They are required to videorecord the real-life experience, then produce a multimedia report in Chinese and share the experience with the class. Lower-level students may work on this project with a classmate, while higher-level students are expected to work by themselves. Regardless of the type of task chosen, the topic should be consistent with class content and, if necessary, supplemented with facilitative materials to ensure access to language resources consonant with students' abilities.

According to sociocultural theory, language learning is mediated by various artifacts or materials used in meaningful activities in which learners are engaged. Aligning with the learning tasks, both authentic raw materials (such as street signs, posters, TV show clips, or social media postings) and mediated materials (such as translation exercises) should be adopted to assist learners' perception and action. A sociocultural and ecological perspective does not, however, exclude materials focused on linguistic form, such as grammar sheets, because these afford development of a deeper level of understanding of linguistic structures and functions.

Structure of Teacher-Student Interaction

Teacher-centered instruction, common in study abroad programs in China, tends to ignore students' individual learning needs. Particularly when language instructors and tutors in study abroad programs lack prior contact with their learners, attention to each student's ZPD will improve interactions and accelerate progress.

Ali Aljaafreh and Lantolf's regulatory scale offers guidance for effective feedback to students at distinct proficiency levels (470). Three steps aid in implementing the regulatory scale in a study abroad program. First, before students arrive at the study abroad site, tutors and language instructors receive training on how to provide contingent assistance to, and conduct dialogic interaction with, students in or outside of class. A training handout is provided that is based on Aljaafreh and Lantolf's regulatory scale (see appendix). Second, instructors and tutors are required to follow the scaffolding principles introduced in the training in all interactions with students throughout the program, closely abiding by learners' levels and offering contingent assistance. Third, the tutors and language instructors meet as a group every other week during the program to share observations of students' learning behaviors and to exchange ideas about effective scaffolding practices.

Effective scaffolding is inseparable from active student engagement. Language instructors and tutors should note which aspects of communicative competence intrigue their students. The focus of teacher-student interaction can be shifted and shuffled accordingly (e.g., from accuracy of forms to fluency of communication) to stimulate students' agency.

The ecological and sociocultural perspective has only been introduced to the field of SLA in recent years. Its application is still at the incipient stage in second-language pedagogy generally, let alone in a study abroad program. But, as soaring numbers of educators and administrators show interest in building study abroad programs in mainland China, the limitations of the current pedagogies of rote memorization and teacher-centered instruction will be even more widely recognized than they are now. As a result, the ecological and sociocultural perspectives of SLA, stressing the oral

communicative skills needed in meaningful social activities, will undoubt-
edly shape both micro-level pedagogy and macro-level curriculum design.

APPENDIX: SCAFFOLDING TRAINING HANDOUT

一：渐进式交流的基本原则：

了解你的美国学生的中文水平：在交流时观察并分析你的学生在词汇，或句
　　法各方面的强势和弱势。在发现他/她在弱势方面有所进步时，及时表扬
　　进步（任何时候都用中文表扬）；

不断鼓励你的学生用中文表达自己的想法；

使用渐进式辅导技巧：根据学生的水平及交流话题，提供必要的辅导来帮助
　　他／她使用更丰富更地道的中文来交流。比如，在学生完全不知道怎么表
　　达自己时，提供一些词汇提示，或者给一个类似的范例，然后鼓励学生用
　　简单的方式表达他/她想表达的意思。如果学生能够表达自己但重复出现
　　某种句法错误，帮助他/她解释并纠正错误。

二：对词汇及语法错误的辅导技巧：你的学生跟你用中文交流时会犯各种词
　　汇或者语法错误。当他们出现错误时，根据他们的水平，你可以提供不同
　　的帮助以帮助他们能自主地道地使用中文表达自己。注意：你的学生的写
　　作水平在这两个月内可能会有明显的进步。如果你观察他/她的水平进入
　　到下一阶段，请适宜逐步改动你的交流方式。

	美国学生的情况	渐进式辅导方式
阶段一	出现词汇或者语法错误时，学生不能辨识出自己的错误。当你指出他/她的错误时，不知道如何修改。	直接指出他/她的错误，提供解释和正确的用法。
阶段二	出现词汇或者语法错误时，学生能辨识出自己的错误，可是完全不知道如何修改。	帮助详细的解释，并提供正确的用法
阶段三	出现词汇或者语法错误时，学生能辨识错误，但不能确信如何改正自己的错误。	提供相关的提示，帮助学生找到正确的用法。
阶段四	出现词汇或者语法错误时，学生能辨识自己的错误，并能自己改正，但不能完全确信。	如果注意到学生的用法有时正确，有时不正确，肯定学生正确的用法。
阶段五	学生基本没有明显的词汇使用不当或语法错误。	正常与学生交流。

English Translation

1. General Guidelines

Understand your American student's Chinese-language level: analyze competence by gauging vocabulary and observing grammatical proficiency.

Encourage your American student's Chinese-language use: frequently encourage the student to express thoughts in Chinese, even with mistakes, and acknowledge progress with compliments.

Scaffold your American student's Chinese-language use: provide appropriate assistance based on the student's proficiency. For example, to help a student progress from simple phrases to full sentences, provide additional vocabulary and simple sentence structures and encourage your student to make similar sentences.

2. Scaffolding Strategies

Your American student will inevitably make mistakes. Use your student's response to the mistakes to determine the appropriate level of scaffolding from the table below.

	Student's Situation	*Scaffolding Strategy*
Level 1	Student does not notice error or know how to correct it.	Point out errors, provide detailed explanation, and demonstrate correct usage.
Level 2	Student notices error but does not know how to correct it.	Provide detailed explanation and demonstrate correct usage.
Level 3	Student notices error but can only correct it with your help.	Provide implicit hint rather than explicit correction to induce student to discover correct usage.
Level 4	Student notices error and is able to correct it, but your confirmation is needed.	Provide confirmation.
Level 5	Student can use Chinese to appropriately express ideas. No extra help is needed.	Maintain the communication.

The City as the Classroom: Maximizing Learning Abroad through Language and Culture Experiential Strategies

Tania Convertini

Winter in Rome

It is a warm winter morning in Campo dei Fiori. People are lined up at the Forno to get their slices of *pizza bianca*. The vendors of the outdoor market take over the piazza as they do every morning, filling their stalls with fresh fruit and vegetables and transforming the scene into a colorful feast. A school group walks through the square, filling the air with children's voices. The locals go about their day impeccably dressed, smoking and talking on their phones. The restaurants and cafés are crowded with tourists chatting, reading newspapers, sipping cappuccinos, or just taking in the warm February sun. My students are sitting quietly on the steps of the Giordano Bruno statue, immersed in their writing exercise. They are observing the piazza, capturing a moment, a conversation, a color, a sound, a smell—and challenging themselves to transfer their impressions into Italian words.

On the first day of the program in Rome, each student received a *quadernetto rosso*—a red notebook—with a handwritten literary quote on its first page as a reminder that literature talks about the people we meet every day on the street and the places we see on our way to school. The *quadernetto rosso* is a reflection companion, a space for capturing and documenting students' exploration of Rome, and with it the process of learning and discovery. I invite students to record moments, images, lines of text, stories, anything from which they are learning in the program; even the act of swiping left or right on the local *Tinder* could find space in their *quadernetti*. The notebook is a meta-assignment spanning the entire program. Looking back through their impressions and reflections, students will be making sense of the experiences that constructed their learning.

I look at my students, engaged in their writing and mindful of their surroundings, and I consider what makes their experience so different from that of the tourists sitting at the cafés around us. The answer may seem simple—my students are completing an assignment; the others are just enjoying themselves—but it is more complicated than that. Everyone in the piazza this morning is experiencing something, whether it is the taste of a cappuccino or their view of the beauty that surrounds them, but my students are intentionally making that experience part of their learning. John Dewey noted that experience in itself is not educational (25) and that "observation alone is not enough. We have to understand the *significance* of what we see, hear, and touch" (68). My students are not only observing the scene but deliberately focusing their attention on a particular moment, person, or story. They find words in a foreign language to describe the scene and reflect on what and how they learn, engaging in a metacognitive process. As Dewey suggests, "Activity that is not checked by observation of what follows from it may be temporarily enjoyed. But intellectually it leads nowhere. It does not provide knowledge about the situations in which action occurs nor does it lead to clarification and expansion of ideas" (87). Through a series of assignments and activities that promote reflection and deep learning, Dartmouth's Advanced Language Study Abroad (LSA+) Program in Rome dispels the misconception that, in order to learn and be transformed by contact with a new culture, it is sufficient merely to live abroad. It is only through intentionality and reflection that study abroad becomes transformative learning, changing how students view themselves and the world.

Dartmouth LSA+ in Rome

The Dartmouth LSA+ program in Rome runs three times a year (fall, winter, and spring), following the quarter-based academic calendar. The prerequisite for the program is the completion of the first year of language study at Dartmouth. Because of the intensity of the Dartmouth language program, which foregrounds communicative practices, language drills, and a variety of opportunities to speak the target language outside of the classroom, students join the LSA+ program proficient, on average, at the B1 level according to the European framework.[1]

The program is always directed by a Dartmouth faculty member, who teaches a course (Introduction to Literature[2]) and serves as a resource both inside and outside the classroom. According to Lynn Higgins, associate dean of the faculty for international studies at Dartmouth College,

> The faculty-led model allows for faculty-student interaction, including mentoring, as well as initiating students into the ideas and processes of research. It also allows Dartmouth to create more continuity between the Dartmouth curriculum and the off-campus student experience. For language and culture programs there is an additional advantage, which is the opportunity to send along with the students somebody who has a profound long-term familiarity with the place, as well as with its linguistic, artistic, and literary traditions and daily life; a real expert in the place.

The presence of a Dartmouth faculty director, according to Higgins, not only helps students navigate the study abroad site linguistically and physically; it also gives them a model for "intercultural communication and understanding and commitment . . . . What it means as an individual, as a group, as a nation."[3]

As soon as students commit to the program, the faculty director makes every effort to create a sense of community within the group. A series of information and orientation sessions precedes the trip. At meetings and informal events, and on social media, the director invites students to ask questions, articulate goals, express fears, and get to know each other. In Rome, the director and assistant field questions before students meet their host families, conduct an academic and cultural orientation, organize a tour of the geographic areas adjacent to the school site, and orchestrate a social event to which everyone involved in the program is invited. Opportunities for students, families, and instructors to meet and communicate informally continue throughout the program.

The ten-week program supplements an intensive academic experience with exposure to Italian literature, art, music, and media; daily contact with Roman culture and society through homestay accommodations; and the opportunity to travel to Italian destinations of the students' choice during long weekends and a weeklong break. Two local professors teach courses in Italian culture and advanced grammar; an art history professor leads viewing trips; an administrative assistant organizes logistics; and both the program assistant from Dartmouth and an intern from the University La Sapienza work as cultural facilitators, organizing events to promote contact with local students.

Students pledge to use Italian as their only means of communication while in Italy, and the program provides as many opportunities as possible to interact solely in the target language. Italian is used for all classroom teaching, in-class communication, and written assignments, and for social occasions and exchanges outside of class. This policy allows students to quickly tune in to the new language and dramatically increase their proficiency. It is not possible or realistic to completely turn off English in Rome; while few host families speak English, many store clerks do so, and students maintain contact with their families and friends in the United States. Yet, in a process of linguistic negotiation in which students feel increasingly safe expressing themselves in the target language, Italian gradually becomes the default language of communication. Research on language socialization and second language acquisition has made evident the link between foreign language learning and identity (Ochs). Language, our main vehicle for self-expression, is associated with learning a new identity (Pavlenko and Lantolf). It is not surprising that many students reported at the end of the program that the emphasis on the use of the target language helped them develop their new language self.

Program goals reach far beyond the simple language gain. In a study abroad setting, where students are faced every day with learning and understanding new cultural norms, it is important to introduce assignments that valorize existing cultural resources. Each assignment in the Dartmouth LSA+ program in Rome engages students in deliberate and intentional cultural learning, encouraging them to identify connections, detect nuances, reflect on their experience, and gain awareness of their role as learners. The completion of such assignments enhances students' observation skills and fosters reflection on the impact of their learning while giving them the opportunity to articulate the relevance of their experience. Students' reflections and conversations clarify how these experiences have impacted their vision of Italian culture and made them reflect on their own culture, significantly adding to their learning-abroad experience.

Reading and Exploring

Dartmouth LSA+ program activities highlight the connection between the curriculum and the territory, demonstrating how learning can happen outside designated canonic spaces. The strategic location of the program in the historical center of Rome forces students from the very first day to learn about local transportation and the dos and don'ts of getting around Rome. All three courses—literature, culture, and grammar—require students to explore the city and its cultural landscape, starting with group forays[4] and proceeding through meetings and interviews with a variety of Rome's residents, including host families, students at the local University La Sapienza, inhabitants of different Roman neighborhoods, and refugees at the Astalli Center. Assignments linked to course readings also send students in search of literary sites and personal havens in the host city. These projects require students to explore and reflect on the places they encounter on the page and ask them to make connections with their preexisting knowledge and experience.

My students began their literature course by reading *In altre parole* (*In Other Words*), by Jhumpa Lahiri. Lahiri's memoir, written entirely in Italian, compares her experience of learning Italian to an intense and absorbing love affair "taking place in exile, in a state of separation" ("Teach"). Her successful journey of discovery despite feelings of estrangement and frustration was inspiring to students, who could easily identify with her ambivalent feelings. No other author could have taken them over to the other side linguistically as she did, empowering them to accept their vulnerability and to explore the unknown. As Valerie Pellegrino-Aveni affirms, "Stripped of the comfortable mastery of their first language and of cultural and societal adroitness, learners in immersion environments, such as study abroad, often report feeling as if those around them may perceive them as unintelligent, lacking personality or humor, or as having the intellectual development of a small child" (9). Exploring Lahiri's experience with language learning and identity helped students understand their own, realizing that they were not alone in struggling with imperfection. Reading her work prepared them to approach all that would follow in the weeks to come.

In conjunction with the reading, each student produced a literary selfie. It is impossible in Rome—or in any other tourist center—to walk even a few meters without being offered a selfie stick. My goal was to force students to use the well-known tool in a new, creative, critical way. The guidelines were simple: students had to take a selfie in an indoor or outdoor space meaningful to themselves or to their reading habits and resonant with Lahiri's book. They were then asked to select a quotation from the book to complement the photograph. Each literary selfie was posted on our group *Facebook* page, where the discussion sparkled with interest and a variety of points of view.

The next reading was *Isole; guida vagabonda di Roma* ("Islands: A Vagabond Guide to Rome"), by Marco Lodoli. With sharp, bright, and humorous descriptions of hidden corners of the Eternal City, the author took the students through a unique itinerary, at once linguistic, historical, cultural, and anthropologic. Students were then invited to locate an *isola*[5] of their own and to describe it in an essay. Following up the reading of Lodoli with a direct observation of the city forced them to look at urban space and people in a different way, awakening their attention and awareness toward their surroundings. Taking their walks around Rome, they developed a fresh perspective that connected them with the city and its people at a deeper level, not just culturally and intellectually, but also socially and emotionally.

One of the students chose as his *isola* a small panini place that he had found by serendipity in a tiny hidden street of Rome. He had become a regular, observing the atmosphere, the people, their behaviors, and the owner's way of conducting his business with pride and love. He wrote a moving portrait of Giuseppe, the man he had named *il mago*—the wizard—for his ritual preparation of panini, combining art, scientific knowledge, and mathematical precision. The essay captured Giuseppe's personality, his patient and respectful attitude, his love for the task, and his dedication to his work. The student eventually offered his essay to the *mago*, who read it to his family and friends.

Sending students out into a new city to write about it first takes them out of their comfort zone, then empowers them as observers and writers. My students' work exceeded my expectations. In their essays, I saw a new Rome; their descriptions took me to new corners, showed me new balconies and small stores I didn't know existed and now wanted to explore. Following their steps and their different views, I was getting to know each of them a little more. Through their words, at times hesitant because of a language they were still making their own, I was reading feelings, colors, emotions of the Rome they were making, day after day, their new home.

Exploring Donna Olimpia: Pasolini's Suburban Landscape

Despite their increased familiarity with the Italian language and with the city, the students were challenged by the Roman dialect in the assigned excerpt from Pier Paolo Pasolini's *Ragazzi di vita* ("The Street Kids") and by the descriptions of a suburban Rome that was foreign to them. A series of planned activities with the documentary filmmaker Fabio Caramaschi,[6] an expert on Pasolini's work, offered students the tools necessary for making sense of Pasolini's writing. For Fabio, who, like Pasolini, is Roman by adoption, teaching Pasolini's connection to the city meant exploring the experience of an outsider. Students would understand it.[7]

According to David Ward, the text of *Ragazzi di vita*, relying on the knowledge of behavioral codes that characterize those living in working-class suburbs (*borgate*), "has the effect to introduce the reader into a textual world whose dominant words and practices do not match those of the reader" (67). If the sense of disorientation applies to many Italian readers, it is even more overwhelming for the American student who is learning the language and is missing the historical references necessary to frame the events. Yet, for all its challenges, the first chapter of the novel, "Il Ferro-bedò," offers valuable exposure to Pasolini's writing and his way of seeing and narrating the city. It was important for students to know that there was another urban space beyond the center of Rome and that literature would help us discover it.

Fabio's knowledge of Pasolini's work, his direct experience of the Roman suburbs described in the text, and his firsthand acquaintance with Roman dialect were crucial in illuminating the otherwise disorienting reading. While some of the text remained obscure to students, Fabio's guidance facilitated an experiential understanding of the themes and events narrated in the chapter. The activity Fabio and I designed not only helped students contextualize the events in the urban fabric of the city; it enabled them to see and feel the places described in the novel and to develop an emotional connection with the work.

The first step was an interactive lecture on the neighborhood of Donna Olimpia, the main stage of the novel and a place with which Pasolini was personally connected. Fabio explained the historical development of the neighborhood, which originated with the displacement of people from other areas of the city—some of which happened to be very close to the location of our school. He introduced basic Roman vocabulary that students would encounter in their reading and potentially in conversation during the visit to Donna Olimpia. The students showed curiosity and interest and asked many questions.

The second step of the activity revealed tangible connections between literature, art, and the city. From the school, students traveled by bus to Donna Olimpia, which Pasolini describes as a *borgata* of low-income housing, with "thousands of windows, in rows, circles, diagonals, giving onto streets, courtyards, stairways" (50). They were prepared by their meeting with Fabio to read the urban landscape, to interpret the fascist architecture and the social structure of the neighborhood, and to understand the specific identity of the community. They explored some of the places described in the novel, talked to residents, and heard their stories, witnessing the profound impact left by the memory of Pasolini.

An encounter with Il Pecetto,[8] son of Pasolini's good friend the cobbler, generated intense moments of connection and emotion. After a tour of his studio (once his father's shop), which was filled with Pasolini's pictures and books, Il Pecetto recited by heart Pasolini's poem "Profezia" ("Prophecy"). Listening to the poem recited in the street, with a large mural depicting Pasolini in the background, was a powerful opportunity to capture the relationship between literature and urban space. Pages of the first chapter of the novel, which the students had read, covered the studio walls, adding a physical dimension to Pasolini's words and making what Fabio defined as an "urban monument to Pasolini." Serena Ciaraglia, the intern accompanying the group, remarked that Il Pecetto "was like a passport to that neighborhood for us. We could access the place at a different level because of him. Standing in silence around him, listening to Pasolini's words, made us like his grandchildren listening to his story, made us part of that community."[9]

The students took many notes and debriefed the visit over lunch with Fabio and in our *Facebook* group. Many commented on the emotional impact of the experience and reported that the activity had helped them contextualize the reading in a way that would not have been possible otherwise. They noted the value of discovering places and people so closely connected to the artist; others spoke about their understanding of the effects that Pasolini's art had on the community. The activity reinforced the idea that learning happens everywhere and that experience can teach valuable lessons as long as one is well equipped for decoding one's surroundings.

Rome and Beyond: Revisiting the Excursion

If Rome, with its streets, museums, monuments, fountains, and hidden corners, was the main stage of students' learning, the artistic, geographic, and cultural patrimony of Italy could not go undiscovered during the ten weeks of the program. Students took every opportunity to travel on their own and with friends to other sites of interest. The program also offered academic excursions, carefully designed as resources for deep learning rather than a shift into tourist mode. During one of the planned excursions, a weekend trip to Milan sponsored by the Guarini Institute,[10] students had the opportunity to attend an opera at La Scala, visit several museums, and enjoy the city while meeting emerging local artists and designers as well as students their age. While there was much free time for students to explore on their own, there were also preparatory activities and guided explorations to situate the experience of visiting a new city in the broader cultural context of the curriculum, reflecting on the urban, social, and cultural differences between Rome and Milan.

The excursion that made the most significant impact on the group was the weekend in Orvinio, a very small medieval village in Lazio, in the region of Sabina, seventy kilometers north of Rome. Over the last thirty years, many have left Orvinio and villages similarly rich in historical tradition, natural beauty, and artistic resources to find employment in Rome. Now bed-and-breakfasts, slow food restaurants, artisans, and art studios coexist with an elderly population living off their small pensions, but Orvinio remains a small village of 487 people, where everyone knows everyone and people have a strong respect for their roots. What was I hoping to accomplish in taking my young American students to a remote village with little cell phone reception and limited or nonexistent Internet connectivity?

I had several goals in mind. I wanted students to think critically about the idea of community and how it develops in different conditions and different realities. I wanted them to experience and observe interactions outside the city. I also hoped that two days with few distractions in the close-knit village would help the students develop their own community—relationships of respect and care and attention that would set the tone for the rest of the program. Finally, I expected that this excursion would bring about new cultural discoveries, enabling students to interact with Italian people at a new level.

I vacationed in Orvinio as a child, and my mother was born in the area. I know the traditions and the people. My familiarity facilitated students' understanding of the village's relationships and dynamics while allowing them privileged access to its social fabric. Students prepared for the excursion by working to interpret interviews from the oral history project *I nonni, maestri di . . . viaggiare nel tempo e nello spazio in Alta Sabina* ("Grandfathers, Masters of . . . Traveling in Time and Space in Upper Sabina"), by Maurizio Forte (altasabina.giscover.info). The project collects interviews on a variety of topics including the local territory, work, social relationships, and entertainment. The goal is to acknowledge the mastery and expertise of the elderly. Later, in conversation, Maurizio used an interesting metaphor:

> Sometimes, to find beautiful and original pieces of art, we need to scratch off layers and layers of paint that have covered the paintings for years. With my project, I want to do something similar to what we do with those paintings. I want to remove the layers that prevent the beauty and the great colors of history from being seen. My hope is that in creating a visible space to collect and display the elderly's life stories, their lessons will be made available to many.[11]

While the video was linguistically and culturally challenging for the students, it was a way of establishing a first contact with the life of the small village. Assisted by Serena, students used the videos to prepare questions that they would ask elderly Orvinians during an informal meeting at the Centro Anziani.

The moment the students stepped off the bus into the little piazza outside the arched entrance to the village, they realized that the excursion would be memorable. From the accommodation in little houses and apartments to the dinner at the local slow food restaurant; from the night walks on the village's dimly lit cobblestoned streets to the chatty elderly man who followed the group up and down in their wanderings, the village opened its doors and its heart to my students. The weekend was packed with cultural activities: guided visits to the several artistic sites in the village,[12] a trip to a historic country farm, informal meetings and meals with Orvinian people, and many opportunities to bond as a group. At the Centro Anziani, a local anthropologist, Flavia Braconi, talked about the linguistic and historical traditions of Orvinio while the students sat quietly in a circle, holding the questions they had prepared for the elderly residents we were meeting there. My students were prepared to listen and to learn—but they were not prepared to have so much fun.

Any preconceived idea that the Centro Anziani was to be the boring part of the excursion was dismantled by this incredible group of energetic people who had so many stories to tell, some of which left my students with their mouths wide open. "Can you think of a youth friendship that lasts up to these days?" one student asked. "Yes," replied one elderly man, "I had (and I still have) a very good friend; we shared absolutely everything, including women . . ." Students' questions and elders' answers flew throughout the evening. Being sincere and exposed in their strengths and weakness enabled these two groups, so different from one another, to communicate effectively about almost anything, past, present, or future, from technology to farming to the economic decline of Italy. After dinner, which the elders had prepared for the students, the real fun began with traditional dances, folkloric music played by the local group Vacuna Sabina, and modern rock from the local band Kilometro 22. Students, even the shyest, danced and sang with the elders and the other Orvinians who had joined in for the evening. In learning the steps of the traditional quadriglia and saltarello, students let go of their fears and preconceived ideas; they trusted their teachers, the elders, to guide them through the complicated steps of the dance. Maurizio remarked that this was exactly the point of his oral history project: letting the elders share their knowledge. "The students that night," he said, "allowed them to take back their role of teachers in life, completely."

I planned our group excursions to help my students think critically about the idea of communities; they did. When later in the term we read the poet Giacomo Leopardi's letters complaining that Rome's urban space is unfit to foster human relationships, students made relevant critical connections between space and community, referring to their experience in Orvinio, in Donna Olimpia, and in the communities they had encountered in the United States. They isolated factors, posed questions, found connections and literary examples, and drew conclusions. The time spent together in Orvinio had also allowed the students to bond. Living together and exposing their true selves to each other made them feel safe enough to build a relationship of reciprocal acceptance and respect. Singing "Grazie Roma" ("Thank You, Rome") at the long breakfast table, eating meals together like family, and gathering for a nighttime walk or a morning run all contributed to a sense of community. There is extensive research on the connection between positive emotions and cognitive processing,[13] and I like to think that the critical and intellectual gains made in Orvinio owe something to the friendship and laughter we found there. As my students commented repeatedly in their notebooks, conversations, and program evaluations, the weekend in Sabina taught them much more than they had expected.

In My Living Room

It is a warm spring afternoon in Rome, and the program is almost over. The table in my living room is covered with treats, and the prosecco is waiting in the corner of the table for the final celebration. The students are coming up the three flights of stairs of the old building in Campo dei Fiori where I live. They are excited but also anxious. Before we toast the program and our accomplishments, they must open their notebooks and invite the rest of us inside. Each of them will guide us, in Italian, through their collected thoughts and reflections, making us participants in their journey.

Some used the *quadernetto rosso* as a diary, mixing quotes from the readings with their notes and ideas. Others used it as a scrapbook, filling it with items they collected, from museum tickets to postcards. Some made beautiful drawings of people and things, with commentary in Italian. Others annotated literary quotations with grammar rules and linguistic discoveries. Some wrote stories; others translated poems. One student followed his thoughts and reflections with mathematical equations, explaining that writing equations made him feel safer while speaking Italian. The notebooks offered students the opportunity to stop and reflect, collecting their ideas on the process of their learning. In assembling the pieces of their experience and evaluating their relevance, my students were engaging in a complex metacognitive process. The assignment not only forced them to reexamine their steps but elicited their critical thinking about what had and hadn't helped them learn and where they would go from here.

During the presentations, I take notes, ask questions, make comments—but then it is my turn to tell my students what I have learned. I learned that, while I can share my expertise, I am not the expert. I can help students navigate situations that are new to them, but I cannot deliver answers. Their best learning sprang from self-direction and intrinsic motivation that guided them through discovery. I learned how important it is to become a team, and that unless we work together and trust each other, we cannot learn in a group. Together we learned to listen, making learning part of that listening. I gained a new respect for my students' endeavor in leaving English behind, in embracing a new language of expression with new linguistic and cultural rules. I learned a new empathy for their effort and benefited not only from the reward of witnessing their progress but also from the opportunity to help them with their failures.

As we finally raise our glasses of prosecco to celebrate my students' accomplishments, I hope that these past few months in Rome, exploring art, literature, culture, urban spaces, and social relationships, will not end with the program. I hope that the collection of experiences from which my students learned to think and reflect in another language will serve as a catalyst for future academic and personal research. Hoping, however, is not enough. As teachers and administrators involved in international education, we need to keep thinking of ways to maximize students' learning experience abroad with eyes open to curriculum integration and academic alignment.

NOTES

I would like to thank all my colleagues in the Department of French and Italian at Dartmouth who shared their knowledge and expertise about the program, making available their syllabi, prepared activities, and valuable suggestions. My thanks also go to the Guarini Institute and to Italiaidea in Rome for their administrative and pedagogical support, and to our guest lecturers and friends in Sabina.

1. The global scale of the Common European Framework of Reference for Languages describes a learner at the B1 level as follows: "Can understand the main points of clear standard input on familiar matters regularly encountered in work, school, leisure, etc. Can deal with most situations likely to arise whilst travelling in an area where the language is spoken. Can produce simple connected text on topics which are familiar or of personal interest. Can describe experiences and events, dreams, hopes, and ambitions and briefly give reasons and explanations for opinions and plans."

2. The title of the course is Roma da leggere, Roma da vivere (Rome to Read, Rome to Live). The syllabus's goals are aligned with those of the equivalent Italian 10 course on campus: students will explore and appreciate a representative selection of literary, artistic, and commercial texts; understand the historical and cultural contexts in which they were produced; become more confident readers of Italian literature and more sophisticated critical thinkers; fine-tune reading, writing, and oral skills in Italian; and make relevant connections between course materials and other disciplines.

3. Lynn Higgins met with me on 29 June 2016 to discuss the Dartmouth model for study abroad, strategies, and vision.

4. One assignment, devised by Professor Nancy Canepa, requires students to explore five Roman squares using public transportation. Variations of this activity may include using social media to report students' locations.

5. As defined by Lodoli, *isole* "possono essere quadri o alberi, libri o angoli in penombra, statue o fontanelle, luoghi che quasi si nascondono per non essere cancellati" 'can be pictures or trees, books or corners in the shade, statues or little fountains, places that almost hide from view not to be erased' (4; my trans.).

6. Fabio Caramaschi is a photographer and documentary filmmaker who works and lives in Rome. His documentary films *Residence Roma, Dietro palla o dietro porta*, and *Solo andata: Il viaggio di un Tuareg* have been awarded numerous prizes, including the Ennio Flaiano Prize and the Kodak Prize.

7. In March 2016, Fabio and I had a lengthy conversation about the students' experience of this activity, discussing goals as well as what we might improve.

8. Il Pecetto is the nickname of Silvio Parrella. The nickname derives from *pece* ("pitch"), black gluey material used to make shoes. Parrella has transformed his father's shop into what is now called the Scrittoio, a studio filled with Pasolini's books, images, art, and more. He is committed to keeping Pasolini's memory alive.

9. Serena Ciaraglia is a student of languages and literatures at the University la Sapienza in Rome.

10. The Guarini Institute, named in acknowledgment of generous donations by Frank J. Guarini (class of 1946) in support of Dartmouth's study abroad programs, funds expenses for the college's Italian language programs in Rome, including the cocurricular Guarini excursion.

11. Maurizio Forte is a resident of Orvinio who left Rome and a job as a director of a software company to return to the village of his childhood, where he now runs a bed-and-breakfast with his wife, Simonetta. They hosted the students during their stay in Orvinio and organized several of the activities. Maurizio's remarks quoted in this essay (and translated by me) were made during a conversation in June 2016 about the Sabina experience.

12. Valeria Lettera, lawyer in life and tour guide for the occasion, gave students an exceptionally well-organized and engaging tour of the village, making connections to several historical events that helped students contextualize what they saw in a broader perspective.

13. For more on this connection, see Dai and Sternberg, chapter 3, "Affect and Cognitive Processing."

PART TWO

Content Courses in English

Developing a Service-Learning Component within a University-Based Study Abroad Program: Implications for University-Community Relations

José Antonio Torralba

One of the central assumptions of university-based study abroad programs focused on language development is that learning in the context where the target language is the leading mode of interaction among individuals provides optimal conditions for the learner (Hellebrandt and Varona). Theoretically, this is an attempt to contextualize language learning by placing the learner in an authentic setting in terms of language use. Practically, those attempts have meant embedding university students in countries or settings where the target language is the official or leading language spoken by its inhabitants. Traditionally, this has resulted in study abroad programs where students are immersed in intense exposure to the target language for several weeks through formal instruction in universities or language institutes, and through informal exposure in the homes of local families or in their everyday activities.

Some universities in the United States have incorporated service learning as a way to enhance and authenticate the contextualization process. Service learning has been generally understood as a pedagogy in which students engage in service to a community in a way that is connected academically to course or curricular goals. An essential component that connects the service to the learning is reflection, a process whereby students regularly think about and act on what they are doing and learning (Eyler et al.). Research on the relation between service learning and language learning is just emerging and remains somewhat inconclusive as to the benefits for its participants, namely, students, language programs, and university departments.

However, the data suggest that students are drawing positive resources from those experiences (Carney; Plann; Morris). Most of these initial claims have emerged from university language departments that have incorporated a service-learning program at the local or international level. A study abroad program that works closely with many language departments as well as other departments within a large public university offers another perspective: that the relation between language development and service learning depends on the development of contextualizing knowledge, beliefs, and attitudes promoted by the university within the society at large. This view deliberately engages with one of the leading missions of modern universities, which is to prepare students as active, critical, informed, and useful citizens of a particular society (Tacelosky 880).

Promoting this engagement in the creation of a service-learning component within an existing language-development study abroad program presents specific challenges. In the following description of a pilot initiative at the University of Hawai'i Mānoa, I want to make use of my own inexperience and difficulties to create a description or narrative seldom encountered in the research literature on the *process* of constructing such relationships as opposed to focusing exclusively on the *products* of it.

Theoretical Orientations

Under critical perspectives, schools have been centrally implicated in de-contextualizing knowledge, or removing knowledge from its practical everyday context in an effort to offer it as part of an ordered curriculum (Scribner). Among educational researchers this has led to mounting criticisms about a dissonance between what is learned in schools and what constitutes real disciplinary knowledge, or what should be learned in order to understand and practice a discipline (Blumenfeld et al.; Fortus et al.; Krajcik et al.). Some refer to this problem as the "encapsulation of school" (Brown et al.; Engestrom). Most of these criticisms have resulted in curriculum reforms centered on grounding school knowledge in the everyday activities of individuals. One of the most recognized forms or products of that reform is known as project-based learning (Thomas). In language programs, there have been similar criticisms and proposals that also try to ground language learning in local communities.

Theoretically, service learning is located at the intersection of academic and authentic contexts. Methodologically, service learning dictates a movement away from traditional classrooms and into settings where language or any other skill (math, science, etc.) is the means by which people get things done. In other words, language is not an end in itself. Placing students in such contexts disrupts their conceptions of schooling—at all levels—and forces them to think seriously of the purpose of gaining skills inside schools. This experience serves two of the central aims of service learning: recognition that the skills gained at school (in this case a university) can help others, and achievement through that help of an understanding of oneself within a particular society. The idea of dialogue proposed by the philosopher Martin Buber and presented in its more practical instantiations by the Brazilian educator Paulo Freire can usefully guide service-learning activity. The idea of dialogue as an encounter of the I-You (rather than the objectifying I-It) recognizes two important aspects relevant for this discussion. First, according to Buber, it necessitates an inclusion of the other, a consideration of the other as a person who must be listened to with respect in order for such dialogue to exist. Second, according to Freire, it involves work, or praxis. This means getting engaged with activities that have real meaning in the form of economic and political consequences for those whom one is trying to help.

These two components, while simple enough, represent a departure from traditional forms of learning language. As Kathleen Tacelosky reminds us, students in traditional language courses do not have the opportunity to encounter others in authentic situations where they might be forced to deal with the immediate contingencies of language in the context of doing something (877). In the program where I worked, students were asked to enter into authentic dialogue with local schools in order to recognize what they could do to help the ongoing work of the school. Praxis also provided a tangible theoretical orientation: the program was guided by an expectation that students must not only seek to gain from serving the community, but should also engage with the expectation of giving, and through such giving would come to recognize the wealth of skills and knowledge they possessed and the way those skills could help others. When a study abroad program shifts its attention away from solely gaining to also offering, students engage with local communities. They are tasked with understanding where they can help and how the knowledge and skills gained through university training can be of use to others who have not had the opportunity to benefit from these institutions. Freire's work provides a sound theoretical guide because it illustrates a process or dialogue for changing a particular condition and a process for changing oneself through self-reflective practices.

Methods

During the summer of 2012, I was the resident director for the University of Hawai'i Mānoa's study abroad program in Mendoza, Argentina. Prior to the six weeks of residence there, an existing undergraduate education course, Introduction to Multicultural Education, was adapted to include a service-learning component. The original course had a fieldwork or lab section that I transformed into the practical work of service learning at local schools. Two undergraduate students and I would work daily inside different classrooms at two schools in Mendoza for a period of four weeks. One of the schools was adapting an adult education program to help students who had left school complete their elementary education. The other, through an articulation program, was providing technical education to students who had finished elementary school and were pursuing the high school equivalency credential.

My colleagues and I expected our students not only to gain language skills beyond the classroom but also to give to the local community by making use of skills and knowledge acquired at their home institution. We view this approach as a way for young people to understand the relevance and utility of the education they are receiving while attending college. It is also a way for their institution to serve the study abroad community at large, one that involves service learning that seeks to disrupt traditional authoritative models of university-community relationships (Sandman et al.). My colleagues and I hoped to create a practical curriculum that other schools might consider. Specifically, we tried to understand the parameters for incorporating a service-learning program into an existing study abroad curriculum and to find ways to develop relationships with local schools and agencies in foreign countries.

Data for this study emerged from my initial conversations with the director of the study abroad program about designing a course with a service-learning component; my discussions with service-learning specialists in Argentina (both in Buenos Aires and in Mendoza, at the university where my students took language and education courses); my fieldwork in Mendoza; and reports by instructors at these schools as well as the study abroad students' reflections on their work there. Prior to that work, there were several meetings with local school and program directors to ascertain their needs and the best way in which our students could help. A list of school needs and the skills and areas of interest of the students studying abroad was produced in an effort to optimize the help our university students could provide and, in the process, could learn from.

Results and Implications

Service Learning as Part of Study Abroad Programs

One critical aspect of incorporating a service-learning component into an existing study abroad program is the degree to which the effort is accepted or perceived as feasible by the institution. At the University of Hawai'i Mānoa, informal conversations with the study abroad director and members of the program staff established a shared interest in adding service learning to the curriculum. The option was expected to appeal not only to undergraduates seeking to learn a language, but also to those interested in community service. As a faculty member in curriculum studies, I wanted to investigate methods of incorporating service-learning activities into the learning process. The match in interests led to crucial cooperation in creating and promoting the course.

Another key factor at the institutional level was the establishment of alliances in the host country. I began by seeking organizations that understood and were actively researching service learning in Argentina. Those contacts were fruitful and connected me with service-learning initiatives at the local level in Mendoza. However, we lacked the benefit of face-to-face meetings to explore how our students could begin to work at the local level once they arrived in Mendoza. A list of our students' interests and skills was sent to a university-based coordinator of service learning, and the coordinator made recommendations and helped us to contact local school administrators. Those connections at the school level proved to be pivotal, because when we arrived in Mendoza, the administrators already knew what we wanted, what sorts of skills our students had, and how they could utilize those skills.

Clearly, then, familiarity with the country, its service-learning initiatives, and its leading researchers is crucial at this early phase of the process. Local agencies expressed openness to our suggestions after hearing we had been referred to them by leading Argentine researchers and agencies working with service-learning initiatives. In short, service-learning personnel in Mendoza agreed to speak with us because they valued the fact that we had been referred to them by larger national agencies dedicated to fostering research and service learning (e.g., Sandman et al.).

Finally, in addition to requiring committed support by relevant staff members on the home campus and in the host country, the service-learning component of a course benefits from occupying a central place in the outreach efforts conducted by the study abroad program. In my experience, students seeking to enhance their language skills through a study abroad program tend to be quite receptive to opportunities to contextualize their more traditional study abroad learning through work and personal relationships abroad because those experiences put them in closer contact with the host culture. In the first year of this initiative, members of the study abroad staff at the University of Hawai'i Mānoa began highlighting the service-learning component during face-to-face information sessions across campus and through online means. We were able to attract thirty percent of those registered for the summer program in Mendoza, Argentina. Such recruitment took place within the context of recognizing that the main self-reported purpose motivating students to participate in our program seemed to be the completion of their language requirement. In other words, the service-learning component was *competing* with language requirements students saw as the leading factors for enrolling in the study abroad program. This realization is significant because it indicates that many study abroad programs are still working under a model where service learning and language development are perceived as separate and in active competition for students' time and financial resources. The goal, both short term and long term, is to work toward a curricular model in which service learning is an inherent part of the language development of students who are taking language courses and studying abroad.

Developing Service-Learning Partnerships with Agencies in the Host Country

Before arriving in Mendoza, students were told of the different opportunities available to them in Argentina. Additionally, I wrote and sent a profile of each student enrolled in the service-learning course to the directors of the service-learning initiatives in Argentina who had agreed to participate. The profiles described the students' skills and university majors as well as the type of work they were most interested in doing within the existing projects. These profiles represented a first attempt to work with the local community in the host country and its specific needs. We needed to build this partnership as quickly as possible since our students would spend only six weeks in Argentina as part of the summer program, and new programs take time to work out.

Once the students and I arrived in Argentina, we discovered that it took about two weeks to smooth out all the details necessary for beginning work at the individual sites in the programs we had identified. Even though my native language is Spanish and I am fairly well acquainted with Argentina's educational system, placing our students in local schools serving marginalized and underserved students required repeated visits and conversations with the directors of these institutions. In general, these individuals were quite receptive to our goals but wanted very much to meet us face-to-face to make sure that all constituents could work within the settings and among the people to be served. In short, forging the local relationships necessary for implementing a service-learning component is in itself a cultural and interpersonal exchange that must be carefully and sensitively negotiated. Once that phase is accomplished, things can go more smoothly.

My students worked with two local schools that served students fourteen to seventeen years of age working to complete their elementary or high school classes under a pedagogical model of adult education. We restricted our scope to two sites in order to optimize the limited amount of time we had in the country. We also wanted to focus on developing relationships with a limited number of people (students, teachers, and administrators) with hopes of sustaining these relationships beyond the single year of initially working with them. We strongly suggest that any institution hoping to incorporate service learning abroad direct its efforts toward local sites and specific programs that offer the potential for extended, collaborative, and sustained relationships.

A crucial part of developing a partnership with the local community at a study abroad site is to center on activities that organically emerge out of local needs. For instance, teachers in Mendoza requested that our students enhance instruction in the natural sciences by designing lessons on the water cycle and how pollution affects the cycle. They asked our students to create and implement assessments that explore the academic and personal potential of eighth- and ninth-grade students traditionally left out of the school system in Argentina. They also hoped that our students would participate in the development of affective aspects of basic literacy. These included, for example, school-based breakfasts where students with very limited literacy began to express their desires for formal schooling and to articulate the barriers they experienced.

Finally, it is important to consider that the in-country program and the department that hosts a study abroad program such as I am outlining here may be highly structured and leave little room for additions. I experienced high levels of receptivity to the ideas of service learning and our efforts to work in local schools. However, such receptivity did not translate into willingness to modify any of the local language courses to include visits to the schools where the work I am describing was being conducted. Achieving this goal will take time, effort, and collective coordination by administrators on both sides to see the usefulness of a service-learning component to their traditional language courses. Field trips designed to highlight the local culture do not provide as intimate an experience of the issues and problems the local culture faces as does the daily work at local marginalized schools. Nor do these trips give students the opportunity to speak and listen to the language in an active manner that shows true engagement and dialogue. Students in my education course repeatedly expressed to me the difference between using the language during traditional instruction and doing so in the service of helping others. They viewed the latter as much more valuable within the limited time they had in the country.

While the embryonic stages of designing and implementing a service-learning component for an existing language development study abroad program require patience, there is much to be gained from careful preparation. My intention, in examining a service-learning program in the making and the notions that guided us, is to offer both a cautionary and enthusiastic model for other teachers and program directors to consider for their own study abroad offerings.

How Study Abroad Experiences Develop Multicultural Awareness in Preservice Teachers: An Eleven-Year Multiple Case Study

Suniti Sharma
and
JoAnn Phillion

In recent years, the United States has witnessed a significant increase in the number of culturally and linguistically diverse, nonwhite students in K–12 schools across the country (Gay). In spite of the demographic changes in the classroom, teachers entering the profession continue to be predominantly white, monolingual, and monocultural with little multicultural awareness or exposure to diverse global perspectives, languages, and learning styles (Stewart). Most teachers are unfamiliar with the cultural knowledge and learning styles of students for whom English is not the dominant language, or of immigrant students who speak a rich variation of English that is used in different parts of the world, and are inexperienced in building upon students' first language and culture to support overall academic success. Therefore, a critical imperative for teacher educators is preparing K–12 teachers with multicultural perspectives and competencies for addressing the academic needs of diverse student populations in twenty-first-century classrooms.

The rapid changes in student demographics have combined with a growing need to prepare future teachers with a deeper understanding of international classroom contexts, cultures, and learning styles. Many teacher education programs across the United States have included study abroad programs, tailoring their coursework to offer opportunities to future teachers, beginning at the preservice level, for practicums in multicultural international environments that closely resemble the cultural and linguistic contexts in which they will teach. Preservice teachers are education majors enrolled in a four-year teacher education program as part of the certification process for teaching in K–12 school settings. We opted to study this population of prospective teachers as a first step toward delineating the process of bridging the gap between the academic needs of diverse students and teachers' multicultural awareness, beginning as early as the preservice level. This essay presents an eleven-year multiple case study examining how study abroad programs at universities in the United States that include an international field experience practicum develop multicultural awareness in preservice teachers for teaching cultural and linguistic diversity.

Preservice teaching is an essential experience in the teacher certification program, providing the opportunity to observe and experience teaching responsibilities in authentic K–12 classrooms. Throughout the four-year program, preservice teachers are required to complete course work in traditional face-to-face classrooms and through field experiences in K–12 classrooms where they are introduced to the teaching role by a mentor or cooperating teacher. The cooperating teacher introduces preservice teachers to classroom management and instruction, lesson design and implementation according to state requirements, and assessment of student knowledge.

Current pedagogical perspectives do not challenge teachers' assumptions about cultural and linguistic diversity, nor do they problematize teachers' classroom practices based on normative discourses privileging monolingualism (Cummins; Gándara and Contreras). Hence, an important aspect of preservice teaching is exposure to the changing population of K–12 schools, especially English as a Second Language (ESL) learners, leading to recognition of how culture and language influence the teaching and learning process not only in the English language arts classroom but in all classrooms. Many school programs and policies for ESL learners in K–12 settings, whether mandated by federal policy such as the No Child Left Behind Act of 2001 or created by classroom teachers, advocate specific strategies for addressing the language development of ESL learners rather than challenge the assumption of monolingualism and English-only practices and build upon the knowledge and skills of bilingual students (García and Sylvan). Generalized, prescriptive, and embedded in a language of deficit, language development frameworks do not work for all language learners; therefore, students are more likely to be marginalized from school opportunities as their knowledge and skills remain misunderstood and underutilized by their teachers, most of whom are monolingual (Martínez). In addition, invested in the English-only policy, most classroom teachers align their teaching with the cultural deficiency theory that places minority culture and low English language proficiency levels as the source of poor school performance in all subject areas (Ruiz).

When teachers enter the profession, they are not required to have knowledge of foreign languages. However, knowledge of foreign languages, world Englishes, and diverse cultures is being increasingly recognized by researchers of bilingual education as a powerful pedagogical asset for effective teaching in linguistically complex classrooms. Accordingly, research documents the need to shift teachers' attitudes away from the monolingual norm, toward understanding the multiple language backgrounds of students and developing pedagogical strategies for building upon the language skills of ESL students.

We use Michael Vavrus's definition of transformative multicultural education to frame this study (6–7). According to Vavrus, transformative multicultural education is an ongoing process of engagement with cultural and linguistic diversity combined with critical self-reflection on one's own beliefs and perspectives. Drawing from Vavrus, we define multicultural awareness for preservice teachers as the development of core competencies for culturally and linguistically responsive teaching. These competencies include the ability to question assimilationist monolingual and monocultural beliefs and perspectives; to reflect on cultural assumptions embedded in the everyday use of English and implicit in classroom practice; to go beyond current understanding of cultural and linguistic differences in order to develop the knowledge, skills, and dispositions needed for effective teaching of diverse students; and to consider global perspectives as a critical component of teaching and learning.

Keeping the above definitions in mind, the following research questions provided the overarching focus of this study: How do three weeks of study abroad experiences in Honduras contribute to developing multicultural awareness in preservice teachers? What aspects of study abroad experiences support preservice teachers' multicultural development? The following brief overview of the Honduras study abroad program will contextualize the study, introduce the research methodology, discuss key themes from the findings, and offer recommendations for preparing multicultural teachers for twenty-first-century classrooms.

Honduras Study Abroad Program

Initiated in 2003, the Honduras study abroad program for preservice teachers is organized each summer by a faculty member in the college of education at Purdue University. Preservice teachers who participated in the Honduras study abroad program between 2003 and 2013 were elementary or secondary education majors at the end of the second semester of their undergraduate degree programs. All eighty-nine preservice teachers who participated in the program were traditional college students ranging between eighteen and twenty-one years in age (see detailed demographic information below). Among the preservice teachers, seventy-four were female, fifteen male; eighty-two self-identified as white, one as Latino, four as Asian, and four as multiracial. While several general education programs across the United States include second-language course requirements, teacher education programs typically do not have foreign language requirements for teacher certification. In our study, more than two-thirds of the participants were monolingual and monocultural, seventeen preservice teachers spoke conversational Spanish; one was fluent in Spanish, one in French, one in Italian, one in Korean, and one in Russian. Most participants were traveling outside the United States for the first time, fourteen of them had traveled to at least one country, and four had traveled to more than one destination. At this point in their course work, preservice teachers were not required to declare a subject specialization. However, all of them recognized the role of language as critical to teaching and learning in all content areas and grade levels.

Self-Identified Demographics

Female	74	Latino	1
Male	15	Asian	4
White	82	Multiracial	4

Students Who Spoke Languages other than English: 17

Conversational Spanish	10	Fluent in Korean	2
Fluent in Spanish	1	Fluent in Russian	1
Fluent in French	2	Fluent in Urdu	1
Fluent in Italian	1*		

*Student also knew conversational Spanish.

Students with International Travel Experience: 18*

Mexico	7	Germany	1
Canada	4	England	1
"Europe"	4	Australia	1
Korea	2	El Salvador	1
Guatemala	2	Costa Rica	1
Spain	1	"Middle East"	1
Greece	1	Pakistan	1

*Four students had traveled to more than one destination.

Preservice teachers enrolled in two foundational teacher education courses—EDCI 205, Exploring Teaching as a Career, and EDCI 285, Multi-culturalism in Education—and participated in several planned events for interacting with local communities. The aim of the two courses was to introduce preservice teachers to the theories, philosophies, policies, and issues relevant to teaching in K–12 schools, and to develop multicultural competencies and pedagogies. The three-week program in Honduras included an international field placement practicum in an elementary school in Zamorano. Course work combined with an international field placement practicum provided new opportunities for preservice teachers to experience culturally and linguistically diverse school communities; to examine their own personal and professional values, beliefs, and assumptions; and to reflect on what these might mean for multicultural teaching and learning.

Course work consisted of reading and responding to scholarship on research, policy, and practice relating to teaching diversity in K–12 school systems; working directly with culturally and linguistically diverse schools through the international field placement practicum; participating in class discussions and critical analyses of course readings, field experiences, and preservice teachers' locations in relation to social class, race, language, and educational equity; and reflecting on the participants' own growth and development as future teachers.

Course Reading

Preservice teachers were required to read and respond to two books and several articles. The first book, *White Teacher*, presented issues of racial identity, racial stereotype, social class, and standard English in relation to social justice in the classroom. *White Teacher* is a nonfiction book written by kindergarten teacher Vivian Gussin Paley, who shares her experiences teaching in an integrated school within a predominantly white, middle-class neighborhood that she describes as colorblind, and her own struggles with acknowledging and addressing race and racial stereotypes that influenced her classroom teaching. The second book, *Enrique's Journey*, by Sonia Nazario, chronicles the life of a young Central American boy and his quest to reunite with a mother who left to find work in the United States when he was just five years old. Enrique's journey from Honduras to the United States engaged preservice teachers with the realities of immigration and the American dream, the complexities of illegal immigration and United States border policies, and the concerns of Spanish-speaking migrants and their children who attend public schools in the United States. Preservice teachers were also required to analyze several articles on the principles of multicultural pedagogy and to respond in writing to these readings by identifying key concepts as they related to their own teaching and learning experiences, generating critical questions for classroom discussion, analysis, and self-reflection.

Field Experience Practicum

Preservice teachers are placed in a private elementary school serving students from rural and urban communities. The elementary school, located in Zamorano, twenty miles outside Honduras's capital city, Tegucigalpa, is a nonprofit school offering bilingual instruction to students from prekindergarten through sixth grade. Forty percent of the students come from rural families with very limited resources and receive financial assistance. The school also provides training for Honduran public school teachers and for other nonprofit schools in Honduras. With a no-textbook policy, teachers develop integrated, student-centered units in each subject area for a class of eighteen students. For their field experience practicum, preservice teachers were placed in the school for two weeks, where they observed teachers and students in the classroom, designed and implemented lessons, and worked with the cooperating teacher.

The international field experiences were designed to move preservice teachers out of their comfort zones, engage them in Spanish-speaking school settings, and prompt critical reflection on their own perspective toward cultural and linguistic diversity. The experiences made preservice teachers more aware of differences in identity and culture outside the United States by encouraging them to analyze networks of power and privilege, such as the place of English in classrooms in the United States and in Honduras; by challenging the systemic nature of institutional, social, and economic categories of cultural differences that privilege or oppress in United States classrooms; and by promoting multicultural pedagogies in the classroom. In addition to field experiences, preservice teachers visited a rural school and an orphanage. On weekends and evenings, the participants toured sites such as the United Nations Park in Tegucigalpa and the archaeological remains of ancient Mayan civilization in Copán to get a qualitatively different experience of the culture and history of Honduras.

Class Discussions

Class discussions served as a participatory and democratic format for enhancing multicultural awareness through dialogues and debates on how culture, race, and language relate to broader social and economic relations. The discussion format provided space for sharing thoughts on the monolingual privileging of English over multilingual and multicultural practices, examining the dominant place of English in school practice and policy in the United States, and recognizing foreign language skills and alternative forms of English spoken around the world as valuable in the classroom. By discussing course readings, participants develop analytical skills for challenging social and institutional structures that privilege dominant cultural and linguistic groups, and learn to examine their own social locations in terms of race, class, and language and the consequences of those locations for linguistically diverse students.

Critical Reflection

Throughout their stay in Honduras, preservice teachers kept reflective journals recording their experiences and the transformations that occurred as they developed a deeper understanding of what it means to teach students who come from cultural and linguistic backgrounds different from their own. As part of course work, participants reflected on topics such as Spanish-speaking school contexts, bilingual environments, curriculum organization, and differentiated instruction, and compared educational policies and practices in Honduras with those in the United States. To provide opportunities for developing multicultural knowledge and skills for teaching in today's changing cultural classroom contexts, preservice teachers critically analyzed important issues relating to race, ethnicity, language, and culture, and considered how these concepts shaped the learning experiences for students. Participants were prompted to reflect on how their own cultural knowledge, prior experiences, and frames of reference shaped their understanding of those who are culturally and linguistically different. The international classroom in Honduras thus became a powerful pedagogical site where preservice teachers could challenge power relations within existing ways of thinking and could undertake critical self-reflection on their own beliefs, assumptions, and dispositions for effecting educational change.

The Honduras study abroad program began prior to departure, with three course meetings on the home campus offering travel information and course expectations, documentaries on everyday life in Honduras, and presentations by previous program participants who became classroom teachers. After arrival in Honduras, the preservice teachers stayed at the Agricultural University campus in Tegucigalpa for three weeks and completed their international field experience practicum.

Research Methodology

Multiple Case Study

Our research examines preservice teachers' experiences during the Honduras study abroad program from 2003 to 2013. As a qualitative research methodology, a multiple case study investigates a phenomenon within a natural setting and uses a group of cases, rather than a single case, as the unit of study. We conducted our study using the combined cases of all participants as a unit of analysis to examine how study abroad experiences develop multicultural awareness in preservice teachers.

Collection of Data

We collected multiple sources of qualitative data from each participant between 2003 and 2013 to provide rich description for comparison and contrast across participants, and for the purpose of thematic generalizations that are a key feature of multiple-case-study methodology. Data consisted of individual predeparture and postreturn interviews; on-site focus groups; and digital recording of on-site formal classroom and informal discussions. Other data sets, such as preservice teachers' course assignments, reflective journals, and researchers' observations and field notes, were used for triangulation. Multiple data sources provided insight into the significance attached to specific events across participants, the ways in which preservice teachers made meaning of their study abroad experiences, and comparisons across participants and across data sets that also highlighted subtle variations in the data.

Analysis of Data

We categorized, tabled, and sorted interviews, assignments, journal reflections, and field notes to look for common themes and patterns across data; systematically coded the data for themes and concepts that reflected propositions from the literature and the theoretical framework; recoded frequency of themes in the data; and looked for evidence of transformative changes in the way preservice teachers articulated multicultural awareness over the course of their study abroad experience.

Findings

Several themes emerged (see representative transcripts below). For the purposes of this essay, three interrelated themes are presented to delineate preservice teachers' growing awareness of cultural and linguistic diversity, with implications for their classroom practice as future teachers: experiencing cultural and linguistic dissonance, recognizing the politics of language, and shifting perceptions of cultural and linguistic diversity.[1]

Representative Transcripts

EXPERIENCING CULTURAL AND LINGUISTIC DISSONANCE

"I knew I would be stepping outside my comfort zones into the third world that is very different from [the United States]." (76)

"Yes, I expected I would have to overcome cultural barriers." (71)

"I hate feeling stupid in the classroom when everyone speaks in Spanish and I can't understand." (55)

"It isn't just the language that is a problem, it is the cultural meaning and the implied meaning that makes everything harder." (62)

"I feel increasingly frustrated. Imagine the challenges English language learners face in our classrooms." (78)

RECOGNIZING THE POLITICS OF LANGUAGE

"I didn't realize that 'Hispanic' is a word that people outside [the United States] don't know." (26)

"Earlier I assumed Hispanics are generally poor and do not know any English so need a lot of help in class." (54)

"Now I realize that some of the words we take for granted and use those words actually reinforce stereotypes." (77)

"So does that mean by putting Spanish speaking students in special ed schools are saying No, we don't want immigrants? Is it because schools want everyone to speak English all the time?" (49)

"I never realized that Spanish immigrants in [the United States] are not called Spanish-American but Honduran immigrants are called Hispanic. So much has to do with politics." (31)

SHIFTING PERCEPTIONS OF CULTURAL AND LINGUISTIC DIVERSITY

"Earlier I thought speaking in Spanish is a problem in our schools and all students should speak English otherwise how will they learn?" (68)

"I think it is better to be bilingual than speak one language. That's why the kids here are smart. Not what I expected." (72)

"Initially I thought being educated means knowing English. Now I realize English is just another language like so many other languages." (57)

"I agree with what we studied in another class—that English-only is
forced assimilation that is not helpful to students." (53)

"Now I want to learn another language and travel so that I can be a
better teacher." (124)

Experiencing Cultural and Linguistic Dissonance

Data from our study supported evidence of cultural and linguistic dissonance experienced by participants who critically reflected on the struggles
of immigrant non-English-speaking students and English language learners
in the United States. Several participants stated in predeparture interviews
that they were aware that stepping outside their "comfort zones" into the
"third world" would come with certain challenges and that they expected
they would have to "overcome cultural barriers" in Honduras; however,
participants assumed the latter could be easily accomplished using an electronic pocket translator for cross-cultural communication (see appendix A).

In their reflective journals in Honduras many participants noted becoming "increasingly frustrated" or "depressed not knowing the language"
and "feeling stupid." Discussing the language barrier they encountered in
Honduran classrooms where Spanish was the dominant language, participants agreed that negotiating a foreign language is a challenge, as "an electronic translator cannot convey cultural meanings" and the implicit "values
and cues in both verbal and nonverbal communication would need more
than an electronic translator." Participants mentioned that while a pocket
translator conveyed literal meaning, the values implicit in cultural interactions called for a deeper engagement with the "unspoken elements of a
culture."

In class discussions, interviews, and reflective journals, several participants questioned the teaching of English to Spanish-speaking students by
monolingual English teachers. Emerging from their experience of cultural
and linguistic dissonance, participants agreed that the challenges ESL students in the United States encountered when expected to simultaneously
learn English as a new language laden with "hidden cultural meaning" and
"adapt to an unfamiliar culture and its norms" indicated that "something
needs to be done about the language policy in our schools." Across the
data, participants gave detailed accounts and questioned assumptions about

teaching English as a new or a second language, providing evidence of how study abroad encourages participants to act upon their own experience of dissonance to understand the challenges faced by ESL students in adjusting to the dominant language of classrooms in the United States.

Recognizing the Politics of Language

Participants began to understand the politics of language that affects classroom practice. In focus groups, participants acknowledged that study abroad experiences made them aware of the politics of language associated with specific terms used to identify ethnic and language minorities in classrooms in the United States. For example, when observing a seventh-grade world history class, participants realized that although Honduran students could speak English they had no knowledge of terms such as *Hispanic*. Once participants explained what the term meant, some students wanted to know the terms used to describe Spanish immigrants in the United States, while others questioned why all Latin American immigrants were called "Hispanic" as opposed to being identified by their country of origin. Participants found it a challenge to answer students' questions and discussed the experience in focus groups (see appendix B).

When asked, several participants commented on their previously deficient perceptions of diversity, noting that they had never thought deeply about labels identifying ethnic minorities and had equated the term *Hispanic* with immigrants who are "poorly educated," live "close to the poverty line," and often "work as manual labor," while many of their "children are far behind in school" because they "do not know any English" and "have to be placed in special education and remediation classes." During the focus group, some participants questioned whether the term *Hispanic* reflected a governmental stance of "not wanting any more Spanish-speaking immigrants" or "prompted schools to reinforce racial stereotypes and generalizations" and whether teachers who used the term *Hispanic* "basically ignored the diversity of students' ethnic backgrounds."

Participants also noted that in teaching English as a second language in the United States the focus is on mastering accent, pronunciation, grammar, syntax, and the conventions of language. Most participants acknowledged after the Honduras experience that they had become more aware of different varieties of English spoken around the world and of the multiple language skills of bilingual students. At the same time, participants expressed empathy for language learners, "understanding the challenges immigrants faced when learning a new language especially when taking standardized tests," and then questioned how non-English-speaking students and English language learners navigate not only the reading passages in standardized tests but also the cultural assumptions upon which the tests are constructed. As noted in class discussions and interviews, negotiating a foreign language led to a deeper understanding of the hidden assumptions embedded in the politics of language and the communication skills non-English-speaking students must simultaneously learn, interpret, and master when learning a new language.

Shifting Perceptions of Cultural and Linguistic Diversity

After returning from studying abroad in Honduras, explicating their own struggles with understanding and communicating in Spanish prompted participants to reflect critically on their assumptions about English-only instruction and to revisit their prior belief that when students speak in Spanish in school, teachers are faced with a classroom problem that needs fixing. Most participants conceded in postreturn interviews that study abroad experiences had changed their perceptions of culturally and linguistically diverse students vis-à-vis their own monocultural and monolingual backgrounds (see appendix C).

When asked to elaborate on how their perceptions had shifted, participants reflected that, rather than enforce the rigidity of English-only instruction, teachers need to know how to build upon the diverse forms of cultural knowledge and complex linguistic skills of bilingual and multilingual students to facilitate learning in all subject areas. Further, participants discussed the critical place of language in any classroom, noting that when classroom language reflects the cultural thought process of the teacher, the extent to which students are included in or excluded from the curriculum affects the overall academic performance of all students by privileging some and disadvantaging others.

Most preservice teachers acknowledged that the responsibility of teaching students the spoken and academic language is not limited to the English language arts classroom but is a critical component of all subject areas. In postreturn interviews, participants stated that, when placed at a disadvantage in a Spanish classroom in Honduras, they had been prompted to think about their initial assumptions and biases toward students who "don't know English." Participants reflected that previously they had assumed English language learners were "not interested in learning English" or were "challenged learners" because "their parents were not educated," and acknowledged that prior to studying abroad they had mistakenly equated "being educated" with "knowing English."

In postreturn interviews some participants questioned the overrepresentation of immigrant students in special education and remedial classrooms in the United States, while others stated in their reflective journals that English-only instruction suggested "forced assimilation into our norms that ignored the complex communication skills of those students who are bilingual" and whose skills might serve as a "powerful teaching tool" in the classroom. Several participants reflected that their own experience of trying to communicate in a Spanish-speaking culture made them question whether English-only instruction "undermined linguistic diversity" and amounted to a form of "language discrimination" and "language racism."

Across the data, all the participants agreed that, rather than endorse English-only instruction or assume immigrant students and English language learners are "a problem to be fixed," they needed course work on how to build upon the bilingual and multilingual skills of diverse students. Participants' exposure to a foreign language and motivation to continue learning bilingual and multilingual skills helped transform their understanding of how to teach culturally and linguistically diverse students.

Moving forward, we recommend the following for effective teacher preparation: foreign language exposure that expands preservice teachers' knowledge of and skills for teaching linguistic diversity; international field placement practicums for all prospective teachers for working in global classroom settings; and study abroad programs as an effective approach to ongoing professional development of all teachers and teacher educators for transformative multicultural teaching that addresses the academic needs of culturally and linguistically diverse student populations in twenty-first-century classrooms.

NOTE

1. Numbers in parentheses represent the number of times the themes were discussed or mentioned by participants. Each of the themes reported was identified in data from twenty-five or more participants. If a theme emerged from fewer than twenty-five participants, we did not report it in the analysis.

Appendix A

Predeparture Interview Protocol

What influenced you to choose teaching as a profession?
What goals do you have for your future students?
Why do you wish to study abroad?
What do you think you will see and experience in Honduras?
What do you hope to learn in Honduras?
What, if any, prior knowledge do you have of Honduran culture?
What challenges do you anticipate, if any?
How do you think teaching in Honduras will compare to the United States?

Appendix B

On-Site Focus Group Interview Protocol

What were your preconceived notions for this study abroad trip prior to arrival? How do those compare with your actual experiences thus far in Honduras?
In what ways, if at all, have your thoughts on what it means to be a teacher changed since your time in Honduras?
What sort of teaching strategies did you find teachers use in the classroom in Honduras? How do they compare and contrast with the instructional practices you have witnessed in the United States?
How have you managed to communicate without knowing much Spanish?
How does it feel to be in a country where the majority of the people are Latino and Latina and speak Spanish, not English?
What has been your reaction to the poverty you have seen in Honduras?
Has your perception of English-language learners changed? What is your perception of bilingual classrooms?
Are there any experiences on this trip that you feel have helped prepare you to be a teacher?

Appendix C

Follow-Up Interview Protocol

What initially sparked your interest in the Honduras study abroad program?
Has your study abroad trip to Honduras changed your outlook on education and overall worldview? If so, in what ways?
What have you learned about yourself as a result of your study abroad trip to Honduras?
Given all the experiences you had while in Honduras, what images have stayed with you?

Many preservice teachers shared how being a man or a woman—or a white person or a person of color—shaped their experiences while in Honduras. How do you think your experiences were shaped by your gender and race?

Many preservice teachers remarked on the high level of need in Honduras. What have been your thoughts on poverty issues since your return to the United States? How have they changed as a result of the study abroad experience?

How have you used (or how do you plan on using) your experiences abroad to enhance the educational experiences of your peers at your home university and of the students and teachers you interact with in the schools?

Has the study abroad experience impacted your career goals or the type of schools where you might be willing to work? If so, in what ways?

Active Learning through Academic Travel, Research, and Collaboration: The Arts of Medieval and Renaissance Britain

Rosanne Fleszar Denhard

I designed the travel course The Arts of Medieval and Renaissance Britain as an opportunity to affirm the essence of the liberal arts through transformative, active learning experiences focusing on content study combined with the building of skills, methods, and experiences that students can apply outside the course's subject areas of British medieval and Renaissance studies. The course's interdisciplinary focus contextualizes the literary arts and their relation to the visual and performing arts within the cultural and historical heritage of Great Britain from early Anglo-Saxon culture through the Restoration. The course is cross-listed in honors and English and is directed toward talented and motivated students, with an emphasis on shaping new student work.[1] My intention with this course (and every course) is to foreground active learning in all its possibilities.[2]

I teach at a small, public liberal arts college. Massachusetts College of Liberal Arts (MCLA), part of the university system of the Commonwealth of Massachusetts, is a member of the Council of Public Liberal Arts Colleges (COPLAC). We are fortunate at MCLA to have small class sizes, a dedicated faculty of teaching-focused scholars, an undergraduate population that includes some exceptional students, an active honors program, and an institutional commitment to cultivating undergraduate research and other learning activities identified by the Association of American Colleges and Universities as "high-impact," such as academic travel (Kuh). Since my study abroad course is upper-level and designed for active learning in ways merging scholarly and personal growth, the students I accept into the class group must be able to work both independently and collaboratively with a high degree of responsibility. The course is open to honors program students and to students not in the honors program who demonstrate the potential to complete honors-level work. Often, I already know the students' work and qualifications from prior courses. In situations where this is not the case, I rely upon personal interviews with the students, transcripts, and sometimes the recommendations of colleagues.

Since most of the students enrolling in this course are already accustomed to considering historical and cultural contexts when exploring literature and other arts as manifestations of human experience, many of them will approach the course as a deeper exploration of already familiar scholarly territory. The variety of majors and wide range of course content make for a stimulating blend of interests, experience levels, and learning styles among the students in the class.

The Arts of Medieval and Renaissance Britain's course schedule of a full semester of on-campus study combined with an integrated eleven-day travel component allows sufficient time for the learning process to unfold before, during, and after travel. Academic travel, regardless of duration, should be a learning experience that stays with students and grows. I do not simply want to bring students to a new geographical place. The goal is to guide them to a new intellectual place as well. My plan is that they will interact with each other and with me in collaborative problem solving, using the course content and moving beyond it through research and creative projects. Some students continue their projects long after the course is over, producing creative writing, visual art, small-scale and large-scale performing arts projects, publications, and presentations at campus-wide, statewide, and regional undergraduate research conferences.

Academic travel is expensive, yet it is important for public liberal arts schools to offer learning experiences comparable to those of private institutions. I keep students' costs affordable while offering a high-quality travel experience coordinated with the course's academic and cocurricular goals by making all arrangements myself and by drawing upon my extensive travel experience and contacts.[3] Members of MCLA's financial aid staff advise students on financing their travel, and as an institution we continually explore new options. In 2013–14, the inaugural year of the MCLA Travel Course Scholarships, a faculty initiative I helped lead, thirteen students from seven courses traveling within and outside the United States received partial funding from competitive merit-based scholarships supported by the MCLA Foundation through significant alumni contributions.[4]

Each year, specific events and opportunities in Britain help determine our daily schedule during the travel component and affect the framing of course content on campus. For example, studying a Shakespeare play in class, taking a specialist tour and workshop at the re-creation of Shakespeare's Globe Theatre in London, and attending a professional production of the play can combine to shape an integrated learning experience. Depending upon our chosen play and the class group's interests and affinities, we might concentrate our attention on performance aspects, on language, or on cultural context. In March 2014, during the opening season of Shakespeare's Globe's Wanamaker Playhouse, which extends the Globe's performing season, repertoire, and teaching possibilities, we explored the work of a Shakespeare contemporary, studying Francis Beaumont's *Knight of the Burning Pestle* and seeing the play in the Wanamaker's historical setting re-creating an indoor early modern theater. This proved a rewarding experience that expanded the students' sense of the artistic and cultural context of English Renaissance theater.

Two additional examples illustrate the link between learning experiences on campus and abroad as well as the course's interdisciplinary nature. The opportunity to hear a performance of Palestrina's 1584 setting of the Bible's *Song of Songs* in the York Minster cathedral in 2008 was the catalyst for a study segment on campus that included an introduction to the motet genre; discussion of musical settings of biblical texts in Latin and English; and attention to the text of the biblical *Song of Solomon* and the English Bible as available in the late sixteenth century. The 2011–12 exhibit *Imagined Lives: Portraits of Unknown People* at the National Portrait Gallery in London featured sixteenth- and seventeenth-century portraits of sitters whose identities cannot be authenticated, accompanied by short historical fiction by current writers. In the course's segment on portraiture, the class learned how to "read" a portrait; explored a wide range of British portraits, including many we would have the opportunity to view in person during our travels; and previewed the exhibit online. The exhibit and related course work encouraged some students in their own experiments in writing historical fiction.

Taking *Imagined Lives* as inspiration, one student of literature and creative writing embarked upon a study of the coronation of King Charles II that grew into a researched, original historical fiction project, which she shared at MCLA's annual Undergraduate Research Conference and at a subsequent regional undergraduate research conference of the Council of Public Liberal Arts Colleges. The student explained that the project afforded the freedom to merge history with fiction in a particularly fruitful way. The sensory experience of seeing a particular portrait "live" in a museum set her imagination in gear for a project that merged the scholarly with the creative. Another student who combined historical research with creative writing recalled a moment of discovery she experienced while reading the essay "The Sea of Information" by Andrea Barrett, which distinguishes between the academic and artistic uses of research. This student emphasized how the physical locations of her travels became part of the creative process.

The freedom to imagine and bring to fruition a major original research project that includes the option of incorporating creative work is central to my design for The Arts of Medieval and Renaissance Britain. The inclusion of student-generated, faculty-mentored research emphasizing primary sources is integral to MCLA's honors program and key to my upper-level course teaching. In an academic setting that already takes students out of their comfort zone in as well-prepared a way as possible, it is fitting to further encourage scholarly independence through the research assignment. Students are instructed to use the resources and experiences of the travel component as fully as possible to produce a project that is substantially enriched by the travel experience.

Each student develops a project proposal in consultation with me, and the small class size allows me to give a great deal of attention to each student's project as it progresses, including advance exploration of opportunities for visiting specialized library collections and sites during travel. In addition, since MCLA funds student research and travel grants through our Undergraduate Research Program, I have cultivated this course as an opportunity to guide motivated students with strong projects through the process of writing grant applications to help fund their research activities. My students have been highly successful in applying for and gaining these grants. This helps students financially and assists them through practical experience toward graduate school and career goals.

Since these students embark upon travel with a research plan in place, they are often granted access that is rare for undergraduates. Students repeatedly comment upon the transformative power of various forms of on-site research ranging from specialist libraries to historical sites. An undergraduate teaching assistant who presented his work in various stages at three undergraduate research conferences reflected upon his on-site research in Britain as transformative. In the presence of his subject's tomb in Westminster Abbey, some element of understanding deepened. Since he had special permission to photograph the tomb, his experience of truly seeing was enhanced. He had already viewed photographs of the tomb and its inscription in print and online, but he described the physical experience of the artifact in its setting as a deeper and more personal form of heightened learning as he made his own photographs. Again and again, my students emphasize this when describing the experience of studying a work of art (in whatever medium) *physically* as compared with the more distanced gaze of studying a work published in print sources or digitally.

After the trip, the pieces come together in the form of projects, presentations, and final journal entries. The journals are exploratory in nature and parallel the semester's research work. I designed the journal assignment to assist students with the process of planning, experiencing, and reflecting upon their learning throughout the semester. Students submit journal entries to me by e-mail, and I reply to each entry individually, following up with class discussion and individual conferences. The depth of critical thinking and self-reflection and the quality of writing are often remarkable, making these journals instruments of learning assessment for me as an instructor and for the students themselves. Students also contribute to the development of the course Web site after travel, which provides opportunities for sharing their experience with the MCLA community and beyond. In the form of excerpts and abstracts, the Web site merges the recording and reflecting of the journals with the scholarship and creativity of the research and artistic projects.

Students make project presentations in class near the end of the semester. These multimedia presentations are major teaching opportunities for the students and provide a fulfilling sense of closure to the course. Especially since many students are heavily involved in individual research and creative work throughout the semester, this sharing of work reinvigorates a class dynamic of connection that encourages students to continue their intellectual and social bonding often long after the course has ended. This positive learning community, the sharing of work of special merit with the wider MCLA community and beyond, the previously mentioned merit-based scholarships, and the research grant process can be positive factors in the engagement and retention of highly able and accomplished students.

While the travel component itself is certainly the most exciting part of the course, and the completion of the research and creative projects and final presentations are the academic culmination of the course, participation in undergraduate research conferences deepens the course's lasting impact on many of these emerging scholars. These opportunities have proven exceptionally satisfying venues for the students as they have continued to refine their work for presentation to a wider public. This is true for works of traditional scholarship as well as creative productions. Tyler Prendergast's comparative research into early-seventeenth-century theatrical practices and late-twentieth-century experimental staging culminated in his senior project: a fully realized production of Shakespeare's *The Tempest* presented at MCLA, which he also discussed in conference presentations at MCLA's Undergraduate Research Conference and at the Massachusetts Statewide Undergraduate Research Conference. Devin Kibbe's "The 16th-Century 'Photograph': A Study of British Miniatures," a project combining research and creative practice in the creation of a miniature portrait, was featured at both the MCLA Undergraduate Research Conference and the Council of Public Liberal Arts Colleges' Undergraduate Research Conference and was published in the online COPLAC journal of undergraduate student research and creative work.

Learning is always an adventure, and academic travel sets that adventure among new places, new people, and new experiences. As I intend, and as the students themselves have ably demonstrated for more than a decade, a travel course can be an ideal platform for practicing research, problem solving, and collaboration, and for the presentation of work—flexible, adaptable strategies and skills for the real world of future studies and careers.

NOTES

I thank my students, whose curiosity and sense of intellectual, artistic, and personal adventure continually inspire me. I am especially grateful to Kimberly Domanico, KiLee Fortier, Devin Kibbe, Alex Marshall, Sarah Maust, and Tyler Prendergast.

1. For a view of the course and abstracts of selected student projects, see Denhard.
2. Integrating what George Kuh terms "high-impact educational practices" maximizes learning from the travel-course experience. The course's writing-intensive, collaborative, and exploratory curriculum comprises high-impact practices outlined by Kuh and recognized by the American Association of Colleges and Universities' Liberal Education and America's Promise (LEAP) initiative. MCLA's

honors program courses support collaboration and creativity and are reading-intensive, writing-intensive, interdisciplinary, and research-oriented. The Arts of Medieval and Renaissance Britain foregrounds the LEAP learning outcome of "integrative and applied learning, including synthesis and advanced accomplishment across general and specialized studies [as] demonstrated through the application of knowledge, skills, and responsibilities to new settings and complex problems" ("Essential Learning Outcomes").

3. I advise faculty members planning travel courses for the first time to make contact with experienced colleagues at their home institutions and with faculty members at other schools with relevant courses and programs. It is important to become familiar with the home institution's established resources and to understand the school's policies and procedures for responsibly handling any non-academic problems that could occur during travel. In order to safeguard their own credibility and the integrity of the course experience, instructors must research thoroughly every aspect of this complex academic and social undertaking beforehand, and must establish and maintain clear communication with the institution's relevant administration and staff.

4. The MCLA Travel Course Scholarships are awarded annually. Dozens of students have benefited from them since their inception.

The Beloved Country: Teaching the History and Literature of South African Apartheid

Mindi McMann

The short-term study abroad tour is a popular option at my school, a public college modeled on a liberal arts curriculum with an undergraduate enrollment of around 7,400 students. Many students at the College of New Jersey (TCNJ) do not have the time in their schedules to spend an entire semester abroad if they want to graduate in four years. To address this issue, TCNJ offers several faculty-led, short-term study tours every year in disciplines such as women's, gender, and sexuality studies; English; biology; and art history, among others. These courses, offered over our winter term and throughout the summer, help round out our students' curriculum and allow more of them to participate in study abroad, which is one of the signature experiences of TCNJ. In order for these short-term study abroad trips to achieve their goal of creating global citizens, students must have opportunities for critical reflections and discussions that allow them to gain a new perspective (Perry et al. 682). Our course—including the discussions, readings, site visits, service-learning opportunities, and written assignments—was designed with the idea of not only helping students gain a greater understanding of the specific history of apartheid-era South Africa but also preparing them to engage more fully with issues of race, poverty, and inequality as global citizens when they graduate from TCNJ.

Background

In the winter term of 2016, I cotaught a faculty-led study abroad tour to South Africa with Matthew Bender, an associate professor of history at TCNJ. While Dr. Bender had accompanied smaller groups of students to Tanzania, I was a novice taking students abroad for the first time. We planned on spending three weeks in South Africa, from 2 to 22 January. Our choice to propose a course in the history and literature of apartheid in South Africa emerged from several considerations. First, South African culture provided us (a scholar of postcolonial literature and a scholar of African history) with immediate common ground. Our second reason was the relative accessibility of South Africa. English is one of eleven official languages in South Africa and is widely spoken in Johannesburg and Cape Town. There is also a strong infrastructure in case of emergencies. Finally, the trip aligned with our commitment to expanding course offerings within history and literature beyond American and Western European traditions. While TCNJ has held several study tours in Africa, notably in Tanzania and South Africa, for a variety of reasons neither of those courses had been offered in several years. This absence stood in stark contrast to the number of courses offered in Europe every winter and summer. With the support and encouragement of both our departments, as well as our school's Center for Global Engagement, we offered this course.

The purpose of our study tour was to promote discovery of the intersections between history and literature and to provide opportunities for experiential learning. South Africa was not just the subject of our course or merely the background setting for our meetings; the country itself was an integral part of our pedagogical approach. The course readings are valuable on their own, but combining the readings with site visits and experiential learning creates an environment in which students see the inequality and racism depicted in these books, both as a memorialized history and as part of daily life in these cities. We structured our syllabus around questions designed to take advantage of the interdisciplinary nature of the class: What is the relation between historical accounts and literature? Who has the authority to narrate history, and what differences do we see in literary and historical accounts? What narratives do the museums and memorials in South Africa privilege? Which ones do they silence?

Course Structure

The tour was offered as a topics course in literature or world history. Five English or dual English and education majors and one psychology major enrolled in the literature course, and three history or dual history and education majors enrolled in the history course, but all nine students read the same materials and took an active part in site visits and discussions. The relatively small class size and the experience of spending the majority of their time in a group made the students very comfortable with each other.

The class studied the history of South Africa through Nelson Mandela's autobiography, *A Long Walk to Freedom*, and covered the literary scope of apartheid in three generically distinct novels: Alan Paton's *Cry, the Beloved Country*, Nadine Gordimer's *July's People*, and K. Sello Duiker's *Thirteen Cents*. Together, the novels presented preapartheid, apartheid, and postapartheid contexts and provided an opportunity to discuss genre in the context of historical change. Working with the Council on International Educational Exchange (CIEE), a nonprofit, nongovernmental agency that organizes study abroad programs, we arranged several site visits as well as a service-learning opportunity to complement the more traditionally academic portion of the course. While we provided students with some free time in each city, most days consisted of touring historical sites, museums, or memorials; attending classes; or some combination of these activities.

At our predeparture meeting, Dr. Bender provided students with a historical overview of South Africa from the days of the earliest inhabitants up through the end of apartheid. I then went over the background for the three novels and explained why we had chosen them. We also aimed to address potential health and safety concerns and to prepare students for seeing widespread poverty and homelessness. We emphasized that they needed to use common sense, just as they would in any city. Johannesburg and Cape Town aren't necessarily more or less dangerous than London or Paris, but they are a greater departure from what many of the students were used to. We felt it was important that students be cautious, but we didn't want them to be afraid of engaging with the people they would meet, as that would defeat the purpose of going abroad in many ways.

At the airport, we collected the first written assignment: a four- to six-page essay drawing on students' own research and the predeparture lecture on the history of South Africa in order to answer the question, What is apartheid? Students would produce another research paper or photo essay following the tour. During the trip, participation was the chief requirement, along with a daily handwritten journal to help students articulate their observations and what they were learning.

Experiential Learning and Site Visits

We left from JFK International Airport on a direct flight to Johannesburg O.R. Tambo International Airport on 2 January, arriving the morning of 3 January. We spent eight days in Johannesburg; two days at Pilanesberg Game Reserve, where we went on safari; and ten days in Cape Town. In Johannesburg and Cape Town, students stayed in hostels or dormitory-style apartments while we stayed at nearby guest houses. Each morning, Dr. Bender provided background lectures on the history behind the day's visits. For example, his explanation of the history of Stellenbosch helped students place the farms and vineyards of that area within their appropriate historical context and gave them insight into the racial dynamics of the local food and wine industries.

Though a strict chronological approach to the historical site visits was not always possible for logistical reasons, we felt it was important to begin by visiting the UNESCO Cradle of Humankind World Heritage Site and the Sterkfontein Caves. Exposure to the longer history of the region, with an emphasis on the current political, social, and environmental challenges facing South Africa, provided students with a broad understanding of South Africa's environmental history and contemporary social and economic concerns, both of which would help them think critically about the course materials and their experiences in South Africa.

We visited Freedom Park and the Voortrekker Monument in Pretoria on the same day. We started at Freedom Park, whose vision is "[t]o be a leading national and international icon of humanity and freedom" and whose mission includes challenging "visitors to reflect upon our past, improve our present and build on our future as a united nation" ("Freedom Park"). The park, which opened in 2004, is a highly abstract and symbolic space, consisting of sculptures, gardens, walking paths, and fountains. The most prominent feature of the park is the Wall of Names, a 697-meter-long wall inscribed with the names of those who fought in the struggle for freedom, from those who died in early colonial genocides to freedom fighters under apartheid. Our guide, Badresh Kara, articulated the very crux of one of our course objectives when he told the students that history consists of narratives, and that the story told at Freedom Park is just one way of narrating the history of South Africa. Kara encouraged us to visit the Voortrekker Monument, visible from Freedom Park, as a way of getting a different version of this history.

The Voortrekker Monument resembles a monolith rising above the skyline of Pretoria. At 130 feet tall, it is easily visible from the road and is made even more imposing by its location atop a hill. The monument memorializes the Great Trek, the migration of Afrikaners from the British-controlled Cape Colony into the interior of the country during the 1830s and 1840s. Our guide at the Voortrekker Monument walked us through the Hall of Heroes, which consists of twenty-seven marble friezes depicting the Afrikaners' journey. Unlike our tour of Freedom Park, our tour of Voortrekker Monument emphasized a specific and unified narrative of history. Our guide narrated the history of the Great Trek using charged language such as "bloodthirsty" to describe the Zulu warriors fighting for their land and depicting the Voortrekkers as being on a mission from God to settle the interior. Our CIEE guide explained to me that other guides at the monument are more objective about the history of the Great Trek. The friezes, though, are clearly designed to valorize the trekkers. These twenty-seven didactic artworks were even included in South African history textbooks up until the 1980s (Hutchison 115).

The contrast between these two monuments proved to be an invaluable pedagogical tool. The students, who might have expected geographically proximate memorials to tell similar stories, observed the wide variance in these two narratives of South Africa's past and present. They easily recognized the biased language we heard at the Voortrekker Monument and commented on it in their journal entries for that day. In conversation and in writing, several students paralleled the language and narrative of the Voortrekkers' journey into the interior of South Africa with the history of American pioneers and their encounters with Native Americans.

The site visits in Johannesburg consisted of many traditional monuments and museums, staffed by trained museum docents. In contrast, the guides in Cape Town were most often survivors of the history being curated or memorialized. We had three site visits with such guides: a former resident of the area at the District Six Museum, a current resident of the Bo Kaap, and a former political prisoner on Robben Island. Under apartheid, sixty thousand residents of District Six were forcibly removed to outlying townships when the neighborhood was demolished and declared a whites-only area using the 1950 Group Areas Act. The Bo Kaap is a traditionally Cape Malay community characterized by brightly colored homes and cobbled streets. Finally, Robben Island was a prison under apartheid, most famous as the place where Mandela served eighteen years of his sentence. Encounters with survivors of apartheid powerfully reminded students how recent this history of violence and oppression was. They also provided intimate experiences of a culture many were unfamiliar with. Our visit to the Bo Kaap included time at a mosque, where our guide explained the history of Islam in Cape Town and invited students to ask questions. In their journals, several students remarked that this was one of the more educational moments for them. Our Cape Town guides' personal narratives, juxtaposed with the fictional and historical accounts that we read, helped the students understand the complex and polyphonic nature of South Africa.

We also included in our schedule a service-learning opportunity, devoting one day of our trip to engaging with the local community outside of the museums and memorials we visited. We didn't have a strong sense of what we wanted this project to be and left it in the hands of our coordinators to find an organization with which we could work. CIEE arranged for our class to meet with students being treated for tuberculosis at a local hospital and to work with them to paint a mural on an external wall. The TCNJ students were divided into three crews—one group prepared lunch for the students; one group engaged with the students in the classroom; and the third group sketched the mural, which both TCNJ students and the patients then helped paint. Everyone thoroughly enjoyed the day, and the mural looked great. Upon reflection, however, Dr. Bender and I realized that the visit's immediate impact did not translate clearly into a long-term impact for the children being treated at the hospital. It was not quite an exercise in "voluntourism," the trend that Mary Conran broadly defines as "an activity in which people pay to volunteer in development or conservation projects" (1454), often with little knowledge of the areas they are working in. Our students had spent several weeks studying and immersing themselves in the culture and history of South Africa. This background made them more sensitive to the socioeconomic situations of many of the patients at the hospital. Nevertheless, we were at the hospital for only a day, not long enough to have a sustainable impact on the local community. Additionally, Dr. Bender and I were concerned that briefly introducing a group of mostly white, relatively privileged American college students into a community of ill, often under-privileged South African children could be seen as inadvertently reinforcing the stereotype of the white savior complex. In the future, we plan on working more with CIEE to create a more sustainable service-learning project, if possible.

Reading Materials and Lessons

We had six traditional class periods over the three weeks we were in South Africa. These dates were split between Johannesburg and Cape Town, and we spent three of them covering the history of apartheid through Mandela's autobiography and three analyzing the novels in chronological order. Before we began discussions of our books, we set aside time for students to make comments and ask questions about the various site visits. Often, students raised questions they had written about in their journals. While these conversations were important, students also took advantage of the many informal opportunities over dinner or while traveling to share their concerns, their observations, and elements of the experience they found confusing or upsetting.

Over the course of three class sessions, we worked our way through Mandela's autobiography, *Long Walk to Freedom*. This historical text provided students with both the personal story of Mandela, one of the most prominent figures in the story of South African apartheid, and the broader historical and cultural context for the course. Mandela began writing his autobiography, surreptitiously, while a prisoner on Robben Island. The book, in true autobiographical form, begins with his childhood and tells the story of his political involvement, his imprisonment, his cooperation with F. W. de Klerk in ending apartheid, and finally the 1994 elections. Mandela's text dismantles some of the myths that surround his image. He freely explains that he was never a good student, and he discusses the transition from non-violence to being "given the task of starting an army," Umkhonto we Sizwe, the armed wing of the African National Congress (274). One of the key questions we asked this text was, What are the parallels between how Mandela narrates his own personal history and how he describes the larger political and historical settings? Looking at the personal alongside the political in a single volume emphasized the nature of historical narrative for the students: Mandela's story as a public figure becomes one of the key elements of the history of apartheid.

We read the book in tandem with several site visits, including a tour of Mandela's home in Soweto as well as a tour of Robben Island, whose most visited feature is the cell Mandela lived in while a prisoner there. The juxtaposition of the readings with the museums and memorials created increasing engagement among our students as they read the book. Mandela writes proudly about moving into his home with his first wife, Evelyn (104). Later, at the same home, he was arrested in front of his family (199). Our class toured Mandela's home the day before we discussed the first third of the autobiography, and I heard students commenting that being in his home enhanced the reading and made them feel more invested in his story. Students also made several connections between Mandela's autobiography and the novels we read, considering the role of Bantu homelands in the novels, the role of politics and law in buttressing oppression, and the limits placed on nonwhite citizens within South Africa under apartheid.

Alan Paton's *Cry, the Beloved Country*, published just before the election of the National Party in 1948 and the creation of the apartheid state, provides a preapartheid narrative, but one that underscores the inequalities that existed in the state primarily as a consequence of colonialism and industrialization in Johannesburg. Paton follows the journey of Stephen Kumalo as he goes to Johannesburg to find his missing son and sister, and the novel goes on to chronicle Kumalo's responses to his son's murder trial. Our discussion of the text highlighted the contrast between the rural and religious Ndotsheni and the industrialized and corrupt city of Johannesburg. We also focused on the recurring theme of the "broken" tribe (36). For Paton, the tribe is not a specific indigenous group, such as the Xhosa or Zulu, but the larger community of black South Africans. Both urban and rural scenes in Paton's novel explore the threat that industrialization poses to the traditional values of the tribe. Finally, a central theme of the novel is the question of justice, set up in Absalom's murder trial. We returned to the theme of justice in broader discussions about reconciliation in postapartheid South Africa. Students responded most positively to this novel, in part because of the three it was the most comfortably realist. Both other novels, as we shall see, required the students to embrace an alternative view of history and reality.

We concluded our Johannesburg class sessions with a discussion of Nadine Gordimer's *July's People*. Gordimer speculates on a revolution that displaces the privileged, white Smales family, who must hide in their servant's village to save their lives. In the village, part of a Bantu homeland, the family is completely dependent upon the servant, July. Our conversation focused on the novel's form and on how the modernist approach, which the students found more difficult than Paton's realism, worked with Gordimer's goal of defamiliarizing experiences. Additionally, we discussed how the reversals of privilege that occur throughout the novel result in existential anxiety for the characters. Bam Smales wonders privately, for example, when talking with the chief, "Us and Them. Who is us, now, and who them?" (117). We also looked at how access to resources, signified most notably by the keys to the bakkie, illustrates power shifts in this fictional revolution and ultimately reveals the Smales family's shallow liberalism. Gordimer's novel insists upon exposing and reversing the hierarchies and binaries present in apartheid South Africa in order to illustrate how power works. Finally, we addressed the Smales family's metamorphosis. This experience alters everyone, from the children, who adapt easily to living in the rural village, to the adults, who struggle with their new reality. Specifically, we see how the loss of privilege shakes the adult characters to their very core. The final scene led to a rich discussion of whether Maureen Smales is running toward her salvation or her death, as well as her possible indifference toward either fate.

Students enjoyed the third novel, K. Sello Duiker's *Thirteen Cents*, the least. Even though it was formally easier than Gordimer's text, the subject matter, which includes the sexual and economic exploitation of Azure, the young protagonist, made students uncomfortable, as many of them noted in their journals. Duiker also utilizes aspects of magical realism, a genre many of the students didn't know well. We discussed this novel, the only text that addressed postapartheid South African culture, in our final class meeting. We chose the book because it never mentions the word *apartheid* and instead depicts South Africa as a society facing different challenges, even as they're rooted in the inequalities cemented by apartheid. *Thirteen Cents* allowed us to discuss magical realism as a formal choice that non-Western writers often make to challenge the realism of novels like Paton's. Duiker's use of untranslated Afrikaans, Zulu, and Xhosa, as well as slang terms, opened up a conversation about the plurality of languages and cultural identities at work in South Africa in a way the previous novels had not done. Finally, this novel fostered self-reflection on our views of South Africa, and of Cape Town in particular. Duiker reveals the darker side of life in Cape Town, which we rarely saw on our guided tours. This isn't to say that students had a naïve sense of South Africa over the course of the three weeks. They saw the inequality, poverty, and homelessness in the country. Azure's narrative, though, provides a chance to think about the ethics of engagement more thoroughly. While we all saw the poor and homeless people in Johannesburg and Cape Town, theirs remained an untold story, overshadowed by the beautiful setting, until we read this novel. I regularly teach difficult and often sensitive material, and I tell students that these uncomfortable stories need to be told in order to convey a fuller understanding of lives so different from our own. The timing of teaching this novel also worked out very well. The novel depicts Azure climbing Table Mountain twice, at one point crawling on his hands and knees to get out of Cape Town (182). On the morning of our discussion, the students also hiked Table Mountain, a demanding trek. This experience helped them understand a bit more the desperation that drove Azure away from the city.

Assignments

Beyond their required participation, students were given two major assignments. The first was a handwritten journal reflecting on each day's events, experiences, and readings. We asked students to use a notebook because we didn't want to require them to travel with a computer (and in fact actively discouraged it), and because writing by hand encourages more thoughtful reflection and engagement (see Bassot 32–33; Mangen). Students wrote daily entries of 250–300 words and were required to address each of the books we read in at least one entry. Dr. Bender and I collected the journals after the first week to make sure students understood the assignment and were not merely summarizing their experiences but actively reflecting on them. We provided oral feedback when appropriate but opted not to mark the journals. We thought of the journals not only as an assignment but also as a memento of the trip, and we felt that marginal comments would take away from the students' own record of the experience.

While the students met the requirements laid out in the syllabus, several really embraced the journal as a way of thinking about all aspects of the trip. They not only analyzed and reflected on the texts and site visits but also kept records of their meals, how they felt when they woke up, how many miles they ran, etc. This meticulous approach seemed to encourage more reflection and writing in general, and those same students often produced the most analytical and detailed insight into the texts and museums. The journals also provided students with space to articulate aspects of South African culture they found upsetting or disturbing, such as the structural inequalities they encountered (most notably the omnipresence of black domestic laborers in predominantly white leisure spaces), and to explore and process the emotional toll the site visits may have had on them.

The one weakness we saw across the board was a lack of extensive engagement with the course texts. More often than not, reflections on the readings were buried in larger observations and sometimes mentioned only in passing. While some students corrected this shortcoming based on our comments, others did not. In the future, we will ask students to engage more explicitly with the texts at greater length or to write additional short papers on the readings. Separating the two writing assignments will make it clearer to students what is required for each.

The second major assignment of the course was the students' final project. Given the choice of doing a traditional research essay or a photo essay, every student chose to do a photo essay, which we defined as a set or series of photographs that are intended to tell a story or evoke a series of emotions in the viewer. We required that each essay include five to ten photos and a four- to five-page introduction explaining the theme and purpose of the essay in relation to the overseas experience, as well as a detailed paragraph annotating and explaining each photo. These essays were turned in a week after we returned from South Africa.

We received papers on a range of topics such as memorialization, apartheid-era symbols of racism, lingering symbols of oppression, and reflections on the voices and faces of our guides. The essays, though, were uneven, frequently featuring strong aesthetic layouts and photo captions but lacking argument or purpose in their text. Many essays, while fitting within the parameters of the assignment, read as hurried, and some needed more photographs to fully articulate their argument and narrative (only one student used more than the required minimum number of images). As with the journals, this assignment was a learning experience, and in the future we will stress the need to make the essay argumentative, requiring that it have a strong analytical thesis rather than a descriptive point.

The landscape and attractions of South Africa in the twenty-first century can be quite easy to navigate, but the history one encounters on such a trip rarely is. Over the course of three weeks, students came face-to-face with realities of inequality and racism that challenged their understanding of history as something that is in the past, as opposed to something that continues to radically affect the present. In the course of meeting the survivors of apartheid, of seeing the relics of that system as well as its ongoing effects, students recognize that none of the questions I posed at the beginning of this paper has a simple answer. All history is a narrative, and students who experience the polyphonic nature of life and culture in South Africa are challenged to understand how such diverse and disparate stories can coexist. The course never sought to reconcile all these voices; rather, our goal was to give students the chance to hear them and to acknowledge the importance of allowing each of them to tell their story.

Expanding the Study Abroad Curriculum: A Case Study in Mathematics

Monique Chyba

Study abroad is an ideal platform for empowering a mathematician as scholar and instructor, beyond the traditional opportunities offered by a home institution. However, mathematicians are traditionally not inclined to study abroad.[1] Study abroad is frequently viewed as a distraction from career development and as more relevant to languages, linguistics, literature, arts, and the humanities than to the natural sciences. But mathematics is a universal language and therefore should be naturally embraced as a popular component of study abroad programs. Indeed, Galileo Galilei himself said, "The great book of nature can be read only by those who know the language in which it was written. And this language is Mathematics" ("Galileo Galilei"). In *Einstein's Heroes: Imagining the World through the Language of Mathematics*, Robyn Arianrhod describes the language of mathematics as a miraculous provider of superpowers, such as the ability to see the invisible and to travel in a time machine. As with any other language, there exists a grammar; in particular, advanced mathematics is communicated through mathematical sentences with complex grammatical structures.[2]

I was lucky to be the University of Hawai'i study abroad resident director at the American Business School in Paris for the spring semester of 2014, and the goal of this essay, based on that experience, is twofold. A first objective is to present ideas for mathematics course development in the context of study abroad, and thus to stimulate others to think about expanding their own school's overseas curriculum. A second objective is to demonstrate the benefits of study abroad participation for faculty members' professional development.

Empowered Instruction

Teaching mathematics comprises two main aspects. A first mission is to equip students with the ability to explore, investigate, imagine, and create. A second, equally important mission is to teach the language of mathematics (there is, for instance, a very precise algebraic syntax that dictates how to write an equation). Both aspects are critical in a student's progress toward more sophisticated mathematics. Study abroad presents a unique opportunity to revisit these objectives and to develop fresh approaches. Students tend to find mathematics instruction rigid, abstract, and difficult. The field suffers from this negative perception, which prevents students from embracing mathematics for what it is: creative, beautiful, exciting, and even fun. Innovative ideas are essential in mathematics instruction, but high professorial workload typically prevents their taking priority at the home institution. Study abroad gives instructors time and opportunity to delve into their own experience and reflections as they create courses that capture the spirit of the program's location. Each destination has its own beauty and peculiarities, and the curriculum must reflect those; yet most of the work done on a course curriculum for a study abroad program can be adapted for use at the home institution.

At the American Business School, I was assigned to teach two courses: a precalculus course (Math 120) designed to introduce students to tools needed in economics, accounting, marketing, and statistics; and Survey of Mathematics (Math 100), a terminal course covering topics from the major areas of study that make up mathematics, which does not prepare the students for precalculus or any other mathematics course. I quickly realized that flexibility is a key word when designing courses in a study abroad program. The roster for Math 100 was full, and the first day of class revealed that, apart from the students from my home institution, seventeen students from the American Business School had enrolled expecting an advanced mathematics class that incorporated economics. Compromise had to be found instantly, and we agreed on a new course (Math 499) that would expose students to the historical development of mathematical techniques and ideas and their applications in the sciences, with a special focus on economics. The outcome was an extraordinary experience that could not have occurred outside the heterogeneous environment of a study abroad program.

Math 120

In theory, the precalculus course offered little space for creativity, as the curriculum had already been established by the host institution, and I was shadowing a local instructor. However, the small class size gave me the opportunity to revise the curriculum to enhance the students' experience, creating special sessions devoted to the city's magnificent monuments. Learning about the history of the Eiffel Tower was a first step for the students in their encounter with this technological marvel, one of the most recognizable monuments in the world.[3] The mathematics of this spectacular tower can be explored at many levels. For our precalculus course, the idea was to shift the focus of the notion of functions, graphs, and derivatives away from the familiar classroom setting and put it into a real and historical context that students could admire on-site and relate to in a concrete way. The mathematics suddenly escaped the rigidity of the curriculum to become a living entity that the students could experience more directly. The invitation to use correct mathematical terms—increasing and decreasing slopes, maximum and minimum values, and equidistant and congruent triangles—to describe the sight helped reveal not only how rarely the students were asked to speak this language but also how much of this vocabulary is used in economics courses. A more advanced class might study the effects of the wind at high altitudes (key to French engineer Gustave Eiffel in the design of his monument) and the work of an American engineer who has produced a mathematical model explaining the tower's elegant shape ("Elegant Shape").

Another local treasure that harbors mathematical marvels is the *Mona Lisa* of Leonardo da Vinci, a portrait said to perfectly exemplify the golden ratio (Atalay). Using the painting to introduce and illustrate exponential and logarithmic functions encouraged students to connect theory to their surroundings in an unaccustomed way. Many expressed surprise at finding that mathematics was so interconnected with architecture and the arts, and one student's inspired report on the subject prompted me to change my syllabus to incorporate mathematical presentations on Paris's monuments and paintings as an integral part of the course. In a curriculum with even more freedom, I would suggest the following: As the students visit the Salle des États in the Louvre to observe the *Mona Lisa* and to compute the ratios of rectangles associated with it, they face another interesting mathematical problem: given the number of daily visitors and the fame of the *Mona Lisa*, security is a priority. How would one determine the minimum number of security cameras needed to ensure the entire room is fully covered from all angles? This is when computational geometry comes to our rescue in a beautiful way that can be incorporated into an introductory course or an advanced course, depending on how many details are explained.[4]

Math 499

The heterogeneity of the student group made this course much more challenging and interesting. Some class members were mathematically advanced, having completed their series of calculus, while others had only extremely basic foundations, up to trigonometry at best. More important, they differed in their expectations about class outcomes; the regular students nearing graduation at the American Business School expected a calculus-based course on business mathematics, while the students from the United States, majoring in subjects such as history and fashion, expected a course on the history of mathematics. Merging these two worlds required a new vision.

The class started with an introduction to ethnomathematics, which might have seemed completely outside the original scope of the course. I viewed this approach as a way to connect students of different backgrounds and to establish a basis for advanced work grounded in mathematical skills they all shared. Our lessons, based on resources from my colleague Linda Furuto in the College of Education at the University of Hawai'i ("Ethnomathematics"), explored uses of mathematics in cultures around the world, from Polynesian sailors to Akan weavers and Australian Aborigines. Following this survey, I challenged students to produce an essay about a mathematical problem with a strong cultural or historical context to which they could relate. I set deadlines throughout the semester for submitting drafts and obtaining feedback. The students took time to grasp the expectations, since such assignments are rare in mathematics courses. But in their final projects, even the most advanced demonstrated a growth in mathematical maturity that they would not have achieved otherwise.

Our lessons on mathematics in early civilizations introduced the Babylonian root-finding method and systems of equations along with the "golden age" of Greek mathematics, including Euclid's geometry and his magnificent *Elements* (529; Joyce) as well as Pythagoras's work in number theory and his theorem on right triangles. Deep knowledge of basic geometry is ideal for looking at the incredible monuments in Paris—not only the Eiffel Tower but also the Chapelle de la Sorbonne, the Dôme des Invalides, the Greek temple just north of the Place de la Concorde known as the Madeleine, the Notre-Dame cathedral dominating the Île de la Cité, the Panthéon, and many more. A precise geometric vocabulary stimulates students to absorb the beauty of their surroundings and detach themselves from their electronic devices. Paris, with its grandiose architecture, is an ideal setting for this experience, but geometry can be made visible in any environment, even in a natural landscape free from human intervention.[5]

From geometry we embarked on a visit to the world of calculus. Studying Sir Isaac Newton and Sir Gottfried Leibniz, both known as the inventors of calculus (Stillwell 662), led us to the notion of derivatives and to an encounter with economics. We delved into the notions of profit, revenue, marginal cost, and demand function to analyze some specific business applications. Linking the students' field—business—to the particular historical context of the related mathematics, within the unique learning environment generated by the diverse international student body, helped create a climate that benefited everyone. I had never taught any mathematical economics before, and I found myself delighted to be doing so. The students from the American Business School in Paris were enjoying this historical "parenthesis," but the students from my home institution who had a weak mathematical background found it brutal. I helped them latch onto the historical aspects of this part of the course (rather than the computational ones) in order to prepare presentations on Newton, Leibniz, and the political climate of seventeenth-century Europe.

Our classes on economics and calculus, specifically the idea of extrema, brought us to the birth of optimal control theory at the end of the seventeenth century. We focused on the brachistochrone challenge, brought by Sir Johann Bernouilli, as a turning point in optimal theory (a field that is key to economics) and as a demonstrable experiment housed at the Palais de la Découverte. During a field trip, the students saw their formulas coming to life through a mechanical device and explored the Palais, connecting with a variety of mathematical notions outside the classroom. The Cité des Sciences also offers a structured environment for mathematical field trips, and the Panthéon houses the famous Foucault pendulum, which I would recommend to anyone eager to see mathematics operating in a concrete form.[6] In December 2015, Paris decided to release funding to create a new mathematics museum at the Institut Henri Poincaré (Lautréamont), which will produce another formidable field trip opportunity in the future. Of course, structured environments are not the sole option for field trips; mathematics is everywhere, and, utilizing properly the specificity of the study abroad location, it is not difficult to transport the in-class curriculum to unexpected places.

I designed the rest of the course around the problem of the Königsberg Bridges, solved by Sir Leonhard Euler, and an introduction to graph theory; famous mathematicians of the eighteenth and nineteenth centuries; and the four-color theorem, proved in 1976. Using physical and historical contexts to engage all my students despite their different skills and interests stimulated my imagination and creativity beyond the typical teaching challenges we face as instructors, and the students' positive responses encouraged me to instill comparable visions and ideas at my home institution. I now teach Math 100 at the University of Hawai'i, incorporating architecture, historical context, and social activities. Redesigning a mathematics class for three hundred students as an active learning course has been a real challenge, but my study abroad experience gave me the confidence to take the leap. Higher scores and fewer withdrawals suggest that students are enjoying and benefiting from this transformation.

Empowered Researcher

A semester abroad is an incredible opportunity for professional development. It is easy to view study abroad as an impediment to productivity and to postpone participation until after receiving tenure, but the rewards are so numerous that young faculty members should be encouraged to embrace such experiences early in their careers.

While a curriculum can often be adapted to suit a variety of locations, a setting for fruitful professional activity requires careful selection. For a mathematician, Paris is a dream destination (Braly). My decision to teach in study abroad was triggered by a monthlong collaboration with colleagues at the Laboratoire Jacques-Louis Lions at Université Pierre et Marie Curie in June 2012. Being physically on-site at my colleagues' university for an entire semester elevated our collaboration to another level. Daily discussions and participation in local workshops and seminars on our common interests proved to be both enlightening and stimulating. I was astonished to realize how prolific we could be over such a short period of time. It is critical to underline the fact that this happened because I was a visitor and not a permanent member of the host university. For permanent members, the everyday routine and standard, time-consuming commitments undermine the advantages of physical proximity with colleagues. Being in a temporary environment creates a drastically different mindset. Study abroad proved to be the perfect solution to the logistic and administrative tangles that a six-month leave would have entailed with respect to my permanent position at my home university.

Another gift of study abroad was the opportunity to reconnect with a young postdoctoral researcher formerly under my supervision at my home university. In collaboration with this colleague, who has held a faculty position at the Université d'Orléans (a one-hour train ride from Paris) since 2007, I have published several peer-reviewed journal papers and presented at many seminars our results obtained during my stay in Paris.

My experience abroad also benefits my graduate students at my home institution by affording them access to my international network. Networking is key to opening doors, such as postdoctoral opportunities, which are essential in the current job market. When one of my graduate students joined me in Paris for three months, he gained exposure to some of the best mathematicians in the world and was immersed in an environment that specialized in his research interest, optimal control theory with a special emphasis on spatial mechanics. He received training that I would not have been able to provide on my own if restricted to our home university. A year after his stay in Paris, he successfully defended his PhD and accepted a prestigious postdoctoral position in Michigan. I have absolutely no doubt that his progress timeline would have been different if not for the accelerated research exposure he benefited from in Paris.

Advanced academic institutions need international collaborations in order to thrive within the contemporary academic paradigm. Such alliances generate a plethora of activities ranging from visits and seminars to large conferences on specific subjects, showcasing findings of extremely sophisticated research collaborations. Intense research activity attracts the best researchers and students, which is, I think, the ultimate goal of an academic institution. As an example, my studies in Paris yielded several publications in well-respected journals as well as high-profile conference papers, grant proposals, and a surprising new collaboration at my home institution. Most universities have great difficulty constructing bridges between their different units; by encouraging international collaborative efforts, an institution is naturally poising itself for the establishment of interdisciplinary cooperation within the institutional system. Research abroad also creates new opportunities to benefit the home institution's community. A Hawai'i high school student involved in one of my Paris projects recently participated in a worldwide competitive educational program, Cubes in Space, to launch an experiment into space.

The burden placed on a department or institution to obtain substantial funding is tremendous, and in mathematics the role of external funding has evolved to be more important than ever before. Governmental agencies, which have grown to be some of the most significant sources of funding, greatly value researchers whose activity reaches well beyond the confines of their own university; these are the researchers who are given preference with regard to funding allocations. Finally, international collaborations make a university visible beyond its own walls, elevating it to a well-ranked institution regionally, nationally, and globally, while establishing the necessary mechanisms for harmonic cooperation to propagate.

With regard to my own professional development, study abroad produced nothing short of a minor miracle. The impact is still felt today; several years after the semester abroad, my collaboration with the researchers in Paris is more vivid than ever. All the phases (application, preparation, implementation, reflection) associated with this adventure bore fruit in skills and knowledge that I might never have acquired otherwise. I strongly recommend that any mathematician consider participating in a study abroad program—and am already contemplating my next adventure in a new location.

NOTES

1. This is the case at least at my home institution, where I am the first mathematician to apply to study abroad.
2. Mathematics should not be seen solely as a language, however; indeed, the cognitive processes employed when doing mathematics should be distinguished from the language of mathematics used by mathematicians to communicate their knowledge.

3. For a virtual tour, see "The Birth of the Eiffel Tower."
4. This is known as the art gallery problem: see Freiberger.
5. Many books testify to the idea that nature loves geometry, including Matila Ghyka's *The Geometry of Art and Life* (174).
6. More information can be found on the Web sites of the Palais de la Découverte, the Cité des Sciences et de l'Industrie, and the Panthéon.

Art (and Lies) in Paris:
The Ethics of
Miriam Fuchs | Popular Literature

This essay, like Monique Chyba's discussion of teaching math in Paris, has a double purpose. The first objective is to present ideas for teaching a class in Paris, in my case on art and literature, with cross-disciplinary applications and a wealth of options for teachers. The second is to demonstrate solutions for adapting course work, course structure, and group activities to unanticipated circumstances at the study abroad site. The course I conceived for Paris is not as unusual as Chyba's math course taught on-site at the Panthéon and the Louvre, but our two courses share pedagogical approaches that, as Chyba says, "capture the spirit of the program's location" and present exceptional opportunities for creative course design.

My course is listed in the University of Hawai'i catalogue simply as Popular Literature. It is a junior English class that offers upper-level elective credit for all students, English majors or otherwise; and when appropriate the instructor can waive the prerequisites. According to the catalog, the course teaches "basic concepts and representative texts for the study of popular literature genres such as detective fiction, science fiction, the thriller, the romance, and westerns" ("Courses"). This rubric, despite showing its age, enables the course to vary depending on the instructor. One professor might focus on vampire novels while another might teach supernatural fiction. Someone specializing in twenty-first-century popular literature might concentrate on innovative texts such as mashups, books that fuse mostly canonical, well-known novels with elements of zombie or vampire fiction. More conservatively, I teach primarily popular texts that involve the art world and reveal important perspectives on art within their cultural and historical contexts. The specific genres may include historical fiction, fictional history, biographical fiction, fictional biography, semifictional accounts of looted art and stolen masterpieces, romance fiction, autobiographical fiction, children's fiction, and graphic novels.

The variety of popular genres that take inspiration from the art world makes the course especially useful in a study abroad humanities, social science, or literature program. Particular choices depend on the instructor's area of expertise and initiative in finding suitable texts. Cities such as London, Athens, Cambridge, Oxford, Seville, Hong Kong, Shanghai, Madrid, Berlin, Barcelona, and Vienna lend themselves to a course that illustrates the richness of their cultural heritage through literature that tells stories about art and artists. A teacher wanting to broaden the geographical scope of a similar study abroad course could choose popular texts with more expansive landscapes, including areas near the study abroad site that students might want to visit on their own. Internet sites make it easy to find visual and literary texts grounded in particular historical periods and places centering on, for instance, vulnerable heritage sites. This type of pairing would obviously be relevant in history, architecture, religion, and other courses that tend to be part of study abroad programs.

The popular literature course that I have taught in Paris, which I like to call Art (and Lies) in Paris: The Ethics of Popular Literature, encourages students to think critically about the ethical questions authors face when blending "fact" and "fiction" in popularly read texts. (Admittedly, the title is also intended to pique students' curiosity.) Where students may be seeking a straightforward art or history course, it is important to advertise this course as interdisciplinary, since popular literature doesn't often distinguish where and when the invented content intersects with documented knowledge. Indeed, the absorption of biography and history into largely imagined narratives is precisely what makes historical and biographical fiction so popular. The structure of my class therefore encourages students to pose the following questions:

What is popular literature?
How do conceptions of what is popular, what is literature, and what is art change over time and across cultures and periods of conflict?

Why do some popular authors use the art world as their fictional or semifictional subject? What larger stakes are involved?

What advantages, and what problems, do popular genres present as a pedagogical tool in the study of art?

What are the ethical conflicts in inventing biographies for artists about whom very little is known? For presenting private thoughts and dialogues that are entirely made up but that leave a lasting impression?

What roles do paratextual materials such as prefaces, afterwords, notes, bibliographies, blurbs, multiple editions, and multiple formats (e-books, audiobooks, illustrated versions) play in teaching a large readership?

What issues emerge when popular texts ignore or decline to document what scholars have established as accurate biography and history? In other words, what ethical rationales underlie authors' and publishers' decisions to exclude bibliographies, works-cited pages, research notes, and footnotes? How can readers evaluate the histories presented in these works, and are the texts produced and circulated in ways that obviate readers' desires to distinguish fact from fiction?

How does viewing a painting or sculpture or building in its original location, or more usually in museums and tourist surroundings, alter one's previous impressions made by a literary presentation?

Why do some objects have significant cultural and monetary value while others do not? And for whom?

How have certain works of art been widely commodified?

How do ideas of public and private ownership form, and how do they differ throughout the world?

How have political events and regime changes affected access to cultural sites and artwork?

As individuals studying abroad, how do we address these questions through a postcolonial lens?

The choice of texts determines the trajectory of the course, the questions that are foregrounded, and the larger contexts in which discussions and class excursions take place. In 2015, my reading list for the course ranged from romance fiction to murder mystery to experimental life narrative. Gertrude Stein's 1933 anecdotal biography *Picasso*, which is a succinct and readable guide to the early stages of Cubism, sent us to Paris sites such as the Centre Pompidou and the Musée Picasso. The bestselling novelist Tracy Chevalier's *The Lady and the Unicorn* blends fictional history and romance fiction into a rich historiographic record of the fifteenth-century tapestry *La Dame à la licorne* ("The Lady and the Unicorn"). Reading the novel enables students to analyze and appreciate the author's embellishing of history with an unlikely plot and resolution. The novel may be grounded in only a few documented facts, but its description of weaving guilds and their culture vividly teaches the complexities and challenges of weaving wool into tapestries, dyeing fabrics, and collectively carrying out an artist's cartoon design over a period of years. The characters, most of them fictional but a few fleshed out from provenance records, depict medieval workshop hierarchies based on skill, gender, family, and community with reasonable accuracy. Few or none of the students had ever envisioned spending an afternoon studying medieval culture, but their excursion to the Musée National du Moyen Age, or Musée de Cluny, to see the six large panels of *La Dame à la licorne* in their own circular gallery was the highlight, or at least the surprise, of the semester.

Other readings included a few chapters from Stein's *The Autobiography of Alice B. Toklas*. I consider this work a requisite choice for Paris because Toklas (albeit a Toklas entirely written by Stein) exhaustively surveys the art, artists, and writers of early-twentieth-century Paris and describes their haunts. Harriet Scott Chessman's *Lydia Cassatt Reading the Morning Paper* is representative of popular novels that tell stories about well-known art figures from the fictional perspective of their documented models or family members. Chessman's book is told, or rather thought, by Lydia, the painter Mary Cassatt's ailing sister, who died of Bright's disease a few years after serving as Mary's most important model. Although Chessman invents Lydia's internal monologues, she concentrates Lydia's thoughts on five famous portraits by Mary Cassatt. Even neophytes to art analysis gain enough knowledge from Lydia's analyses of the artwork to view Cassatt's work in the Musée d'Orsay with deep appreciation.

After we discussed Mary Cassatt's role in impressionist circles, it made sense to read one of the many popular novels about the French impressionists or postimpressionists. *Light*, by Eva Figes, is a beautifully written biographical novel about Claude Monet. Other possibilities include *Claude and Camille*, by Stephanie Cowell, and Susan Vreeland's *Luncheon of the Boating Party*, inspired by Renoir's painting of the same name. There are many other choices—including children's books, such as Julie Merberg's works on artists and Kathryn Wagner's *Dancing with Degas*; and mysteries, such as Peter Mayle's *Chasing Cezanne*—but *Light* is the subtlest and the most evocative, capturing nuances of light from sunrise to sunset as a textual analogue of Monet's achievement in paint and brushstrokes.

Finally, and regardless of some colleagues' skepticism, I ended the course with Dan Brown's thriller *The Da Vinci Code*. The novel holds a singular status, with some sources claiming it has sold more copies than any adult book in history except for the Bible. It tells a highly suspenseful story that sparked controversy around the world with its depiction of the Catholic church. From a simpler perspective, *The Da Vinci Code* offers entry into the Carrousel du Louvre and teaches nonspecialists about museum management, curating, and, of course, Leonardo's *Mona Lisa* and the drawing *Vitruvian Man*. Critics cite the weaknesses in Brown's prose and the errors in Paris geography, but the book's success perfectly illustrates the power of popular culture to affect huge numbers of people. It demonstrates that literature can impact powerful institutions and lead them to engage, at least implicitly, in dialogue with ideas that may be anathema to their organization or their theology. The book might also lead students to a deeper understanding of their own cultural assumptions about beauty and value, and even their religious beliefs. From its first page to its last, *The Da Vinci Code* prompts questions about the ethics involved in blending fact and fiction; accuracies and inaccuracies; documents, invented documents, and bogus documents—questions that help students explore new cultural sites with increasing depth and critical analysis. Additionally, it is a book that professors in cultural studies, history, or even religion could feel comfortable using in a course similar to Art (and Lies).

Films and documentaries that take art and artists as their subjects can also be used either as primary texts or for historical background, and lend themselves to courses in history, political science, art, and film. Documentaries such as *The Rape of Europa*, which concerns the Nazis' obsession with art, would work in many European cities. *Mr. Turner* would work in classes based in England; *Woman in Gold* and *Klimt* in Vienna; *Girl with a Pearl Earring* and the classic *Lust for Life* in the Netherlands; *Camille Claudel*, *Picasso and Braque Go to the Movies*, and *When Paris Was a Woman* in France; *Ai Weiwei: Never Sorry* in China; *Gerhard Richter* in Germany; *Caravaggio* in Italy; and *Goya's Ghosts* and *Goya in Bordeaux* in Spain. This sampling of well-known works reflects the challenges in finding examples focused on female artists and non-Eurocentric art and history. Nevertheless, it may suggest film resources that could be researched for classroom use. Whether in South America, China, Japan, India, or Europe, the goal would remain the same: to infuse the curriculum with what Chyba calls "the spirit of the program's location."

It's important to plan for flexibility. Writing a syllabus is routine when professors take their own students on a study tour, a short course, or even a semester course. It's more challenging when the contract between the home and host universities calls for the visiting or resident professor to open her classes to other international study abroad students. In spring 2015, my university had recently switched study abroad institutions and there was no history or pattern to serve as a guide. Moreover, the host institution, a prestigious grande école that ranks in the top one percent of higher education schools in France, had no experience in offering literature and humanities courses. The French students, as well as many of the international students, complete their broader coursework in their respective high schools, then matriculate to study business and management. I had expected that no more than a handful of students from outside Hawai'i would register for a class in art and literature emphasizing ethics; the school's director in Paris kept silent but probably thought that even my modest expectation was optimistic.

I tell my students that if they want everything to be familiar and logical to them, they should defer studying abroad until they can say otherwise. In January 2015 I needed frequently to give myself the same advice. Each week a few new, slightly bewildered individuals appeared. Students from Brazil, Canada, Mexico, Sweden, and Poland found themselves in need of additional study abroad credits, and previously filled classes and time conflicts had led them beyond the standard curriculum of international management and accounting. Art (and Lies) in Paris grew to be three times larger than I had anticipated and four times larger than the host university had thought possible. And from there we began.

With flexibility remaining the key word, I approached problems with as much equanimity as I could muster. First, the syllabus needed an overhaul. The course requirements remained almost the same, but the original plan for meeting them presented difficulties. The most basic problem was access to reading materials. Students from the University of Hawai'i had brought their texts with them. The late-registering international students were on tight budgets planned without line items for paperback novels or a series of e-books. Some texts existed only in print, and the search for English-language novels cost the students precious study abroad time. Finding access to online editions and e-books, and arranging materials for the course Web site, required time on my part; the host institution and I were concerned about copyright; and, of course, the school's copying equipment was shared and not always operating.

I also decided to adjust one of the course requirements. A small class is conducive to oral presentations, which give students a chance to learn and exchange information directly. In a large class, students may share their individual work more efficiently through journals. For a course similar to mine, they can write a journal that records names, dates, and notes from their primary-source readings, and the paintings, sculptures, churches, libraries, streets, and gardens they come upon, on one or two days per week. Students' entries can include their experiences, reactions, and other pertinent aspects of their daily routines and travels. The purpose is to keep students thinking about what they are reading as they move through the world they are reading about, and to help them create a growing repository of notes for the midterm, final, and final project.

Finally, I encountered a logistical problem not uncommon in partnership programs, which seek to integrate study abroad courses into the host institution's structure and academic offerings. Many professors who periodically teach abroad accompany students to sites and serve as their guide. When I had done this in past years, only one or two additional students had joined our Hawai'i group, and even excursions such as a day trip to Monet's home in Giverny had been scheduled with little difficulty. At the grande école in 2015, my students' schedule of short, intensive business courses made it impossible to find a common time for trips, so I improvised a pedagogical change. Responding to unexpected circumstances often leads to innovations that in the end seem preferable to what they replaced. Students become better learners, and teachers—seasoned teachers most of all—benefit when their usual pedagogies are challenged.

The lesson here is especially relevant for instructors participating in study abroad for the first time: be prepared to restructure the excursions. Students on their own of course may enjoy a basic walk-through of the customary tourist locations. Without guidance, though, they often remark, on the one hand, that they simply follow the crowds in the large museums. On the other hand, they also say that in the smaller museums they lack a knowledgeable rubric for reading individual artifacts and quickly walk in and out of the building. One of the learning outcomes of my course is that students acquire the confidence to explore unfamiliar sites with a sense of purpose and an increasing base of knowledge. They learn how to see because they are reading and discussing techniques by which literature teaches about art—analogously, descriptively, or in the context of plot development, setting, and character portraiture.

Excursions to the Cluny, the Marmottan, the Orsay, the Louvre, and the Musée Picasso, as well as a walk based on Brown's novel, including Saint-Sulpice, second in size only to Notre-Dame, had to be manageable both for individual students and for groups. The assignment instructions had to function as a surrogate guide to motivate everyone to stay focused regardless of the size and potential distractions of the facility. Therefore, I created fairly elaborate lists of questions to facilitate the experiences I hoped each excursion would provide. For example, I sent students to the Musée de Marmottan with the task of locating and investigating specific rooms and paintings, prompting them with questions designed to situate the artists and their subjects in time, family, place, and culture. I assigned them to compare works from different periods, to report their aesthetic impressions, and to compare them with descriptions of those works from our course readings. I also asked students to use the museum's resources to corroborate historical moments from the readings and to identify the author's inaccuracies or inventions.

Instructors need to budget plenty of time to design such assignments. One preliminary trip will establish what is available for viewing and where. Then it's time to draft pertinent questions covering the academic material, limited to a manageable geography and accessible transportation. Another trip will allow the instructor to practice and time the route to be sure that students' progress will be smooth. Consulting the Internet for exhibition schedules is also essential. I learned this by planning a visit to the Orsay a month or two in advance, devising a route from specific impressionist canvases on the ground floor to the postimpressionist collection on the top floor. In the weeks before I gave the assignment, the Orsay opened a temporary exhibit, and I was surprised to learn how easily even permanent artifacts may be rearranged and sometimes removed. While temporary exhibitions can wreak havoc with long-planned routes, it's also exciting to use special exhibits to determine reading assignments and site visits. The freedom to revise course plans, materials, and schedules, and to improvise in response to changing resources, makes both teaching and learning a joy.

No one knows quite what to expect when a new contractual agreement for study abroad calls for a partnership arrangement. When institutions share instructors and coordinate programs in ways that are more reciprocal than the institutional model of guest and host, logistical challenges may increase, but so does the potential for creativity and collaboration. Despite some stumbles, my university's partnership with the grande école worked out well for both institutions and for our students. It also worked out well for me. I was invited to return annually for one month as a visiting faculty member at the Paris university to team-teach in the international summer program. As a result, I am developing as a scholar and teacher in ways that I never could have dreamed. My cohorts and I teach a culture course in Paris monuments and art, French fashion, French cuisine, and French wine. It's a long extension of my customary areas of teaching, but again the lesson is, Expect the unexpected.

PART THREE

Offices of Study Abroad and University Relations

Best Practices for Planning, Developing, and Sustaining Interdisciplinary Language-Based Study Abroad Programs

Chad M. Gasta

In seventeen years as a study abroad program director, I have seen how university students, faculty members, and administrators have come to share a strategic mission for study or work abroad; namely that programs must provide a meaningful international credential that not only yields a more fruitful undergraduate experience but also creates the potential for a better and higher-paying job upon graduation. I have spoken with many job recruiters over the years who tout the importance of developing an international skill set that requires a profound understanding of other cultures and languages. General news outlets and trade magazines report an intensifying obligation in a competitive global economy to attain proficiency in languages other than English and to gain competence in intercultural issues related to foreign commerce, politics, and society.[1] Study abroad programs, especially those with substantive language and cross-cultural training components, can provide excellent tools for addressing these concerns. However, the proliferation of enrollments for reasons other than second-language study has presented existing programs with new challenges. Whereas traditional models, created and maintained by language departments, have emphasized second-language proficiency, new interdisciplinary programs seek meaningful ways to combine language and culture with course work in professional majors such as business, engineering, science, technology, and agriculture (Huebner, "Methodological Considerations" 2).

I direct an interdisciplinary study abroad program at Iowa State University called ISU on the Mediterranean—Summer in Valencia, Spain, which provides beginning through advanced Spanish-language instruction as well as courses in English in engineering, business, agriculture, and the biological sciences.[2] For six weeks, students live with host families, study Spanish in addition to course work in their academic field, take weekend excursions to major historical and cultural sites, and enjoy experiential learning opportunities such as biological lab work or fieldwork, or internships in Spanish with local businesses or agencies. Using this distinctive approach, my colleagues and I have built arguably the largest language-based (and language-department-sponsored) study abroad program in the United States, serving an average of 85 students each summer and a total of 103 students in 2017. This essay will provide a road map for planning and developing similar programs and will offer advice on how to sustain them over time. Statistical research from ten years of program evaluations will provide evidence regarding students' language learning, cultural awareness, and interpersonal and critical thinking skills.[3] I hope to show that a program like ours can vastly improve students' understanding of world affairs while helping them acquire greater self-confidence and a willingness to work abroad, fostering the global cultural literacy that the professions increasingly require.

Background

Goals and objectives for study abroad programs vary greatly based on geographic location, primary language, and academic discipline. Richard Brecht and A. Ronald Walton divide study abroad programs into two basic categories: those directed at foreign language proficiency and those that are "broadly educational" and usually neither require nor offer a language component. "Broadly educational" program goals include exposure to a foreign country, an increase in cultural literacy, and an improved knowledge of a particular academic discipline (217–18). On the other hand, the main objective of language-proficiency-based programs is immersion in a foreign culture in order to enhance language skills and cultural understanding. Language proficiency is improved through course work, planned activities and excursions, and, perhaps most significantly, interactions with native speakers (through host family experiences, exchanges with students at the foreign university, and daily living). I believe that neither of these program types sufficiently meets the needs of students competing in the global economy. Instead, I propose combining the two program types.

Until 2004, ISU on the Mediterranean was a traditional language-based program offering advanced courses in grammar, composition, and conversation, and introductory courses in literature and culture. Versions of these courses still exist in our current program. Nonetheless, we decided to take advantage of sharp growth in programs in engineering, agriculture, and business and to redesign our program to focus on training global professionals to work, communicate, and compete abroad. We decided to connect the study of Spanish language and European culture to the needs of students outside the foreign language program, providing a meaningful international experience that includes Spanish language training while offering unique courses in English in other disciplines. At the same time, my department began a second major option for students in the colleges of engineering, business, and agriculture and life sciences, called Languages and Cultures for Professions (LCP), and our summer program became an anchor of the LCP program and a principal recruiting ground for the Spanish major. The LCP program includes specialized and technical courses on professional cultures (Spanish for Global Professionals, Spanish Conversation for Professionals, Translation, and Interpretation) and contemporary cultures (Spain Today and Latin America Today) while also requiring traditional literature courses (introductory surveys and advanced seminars). Most of these courses were integrated immediately into the ISU on the Mediterranean program.

To improve and expand options for students not primarily studying language, ISU on the Mediterranean offers English-language courses in engineering, agriculture, and business. Our program coordinator at the University of Valencia helps us locate qualified faculty members; we then provide a general syllabus and work with the instructors to make each course more appealing through distinctive experiential components. The instructors work for the University of Valencia, yet the Iowa State directors maintain a degree of control over the course content so that it corresponds to offerings on our own campus. In the past, students with little foreign language training almost always opted to study in an English-speaking country if they studied abroad at all. By combining Spanish and English course work, we have managed to capture a cohort of students who otherwise would not likely study a language or go abroad—and to equip them with international experience, cross-cultural training, and language skills. The courses in English vary from year to year but generally include management, marketing, international entrepreneurship, industrial engineering, biology fieldwork, biology lab work, and Spanish film studies. These courses are offered solely to students from Iowa State or other universities in the United States who are participating in our study abroad program.

The program cost includes tuition and fees paid to the University of Valencia for two courses. First, all students must select the Spanish course for which they are eligible (introductory, intermediate, or advanced Spanish). There are no exceptions to this rule—everyone takes Spanish. Then, for their second course, students may choose another Spanish course or any of the aforementioned courses in English. We strive to apply a decidedly experiential approach to these courses. For example, Spanish language and culture courses use the city of Valencia as a venue for observing Gothic, Romanesque, and twenty-first-century architecture; Spanish cuisine; soccer and bullfighting; tourism; social issues; urban planning; and political institutions. Industrial engineering and business courses feature visits to important industrial areas, factories, the port authority, and corporate offices. Biology includes fieldwork across the Valencian region. It is also worth mentioning that each summer we place eight to ten advanced Spanish students in internships at select companies in the area, mostly in business, engineering, education, health sciences, hotel and restaurant management, and accounting. These interns are usually Languages and Cultures for Professions secondary majors, who are required to intern abroad at some point.

Other program details are equally important: all students, regardless of Spanish-language proficiency, live with a Spanish host family that does not speak English. Host families provide meals, conversation, and sometimes outings in the city or region. We believe this arrangement to be an important cornerstone of the program and one reason why students' language confidence is so high in posttravel surveys. All students also participate in two weekend excursions to the Madrid area: the first weekend, we visit the cities of Segovia, El Escorial, and Toledo before busing to Valencia; and at the end of the program we return to Madrid for a city tour, followed by visits to the Royal Palace, the Reina Sofía Museum, and the Prado Museum. These excursions include hotels and transportation, meals, entry fees, and excellent guides.

Perhaps the most unusual experiential component is the biology courses, developed in 2007 by Steven Rodermel, distinguished professor in the department of Genetics, Development, and Cell Biology at Iowa State. Students may select one of two modules, both of which are taught in English by professors from the biological sciences departments and associated research institutes at the University of Valencia. Module 1 is a full-immersion lab experience with one to two faculty members and their graduate student researchers in marine biology, animal sciences, cell biology and genetics, plant pathology, neurology, and geology, among other areas. This module helps address a well-known deficiency in lab experience among undergraduate science majors. Moreover, the option of conducting the labs in Spanish helps advanced Spanish students and heritage learners improve cross-cultural skills while becoming familiar with the principles of biology and their practice abroad. In module 2, six to eight University of Valencia faculty members deliver lectures on topics significant to the Valencian region followed by fieldwork at important biological sites in the area. Locations include the Albufera natural coastal lagoon and tidal system, Europe's oldest botanic gardens (and accompanying research installations), the City of Arts and Sciences' Oceanogràfic aquarium and sea turtle rescue area, the Jávea coastal natural park, and the innovative Bioparc natural habitat (an interesting departure from a commercial zoo).

Such experiential learning opportunities allow a variety of disciplines to intersect with the study of Spanish. In other words, we have successfully made this study abroad program both "broadly educational" and "language-proficiency based" by merging language and culture study with course work in other disciplines. Such programs answer the call put forth to department chairs by the Association of Departments of Foreign Languages to provide consequential and beneficial programs that meet diverse needs:

> It is the task of the department chair to define the study-abroad experience so that it is meaningful and productive for a wide array of students, while still stressing the acquisition of other languages, the understanding and enjoyment of other cultures, and the difficult process of turning the foreign into the familiar and the familiar into the foreign. Some of the successful models of the past have become less attractive for many students. (72)

We believe that our summer program is addressing these concerns, and today the program counts on participation and support from faculty members from five departments and four colleges at Iowa State: a true cross-disciplinary collaboration. In explaining how we managed to do this and describing how it has come to be sustainable, I will assume that readers are seeking out suggestions applicable to their own programs. With this in mind, I will address readers directly as "you" in the remaining pages.

Goals and Objectives

As universities place ever-greater emphasis on learning objectives and outcomes, it is incumbent upon you to do the same for a program abroad. There is one major difference, however. Whereas a course on campus is assessed on content and delivery, abroad you are also evaluating the quality and validity of homestays or residence hall living; learning that takes place on planned excursions and in experiential venues, including service learning, internships, lab work, independent studies, and special projects; and, possibly, gains in language proficiency. All of this requires quite a bit of forethought. Start by defining the overall goal of your program abroad. Is it language proficiency and cultural literacy? Do you simply want students to get meaningful international exposure? Are you trying to advance their knowledge of a particular discipline? Whatever the case, design the program around simple learning and experiential goals. Then work backward to individual experiences and courses. Data collected through student surveys, such as the statistical reporting presented at the end of this essay, can help you determine whether goals are being met.

A growing body of evidence supports the intuitive view that students make more significant gains in intercultural competence when studying in a country where the target language is spoken than they do studying only in classrooms at home (Deardorff 38). To advance that notion even further, I recommend homestays—and not just because a family experience improves language learning and proficiency. In contrast to residence halls (which are not the norm in many countries), homestays guarantee meals and shelter, provide another set of watchful eyes on students, and offer additional security. Remember: as a program director, you are responsible and liable for student well-being in many instances. Homestays with qualified families can help head off issues that might require disciplinary action, such as class tardiness or inappropriate behavior.

Make your goals regarding linguistic and cultural proficiency transparent to program collaborators in other disciplines. Otherwise, you may encounter requests such as "Can the agriculture students be excused from their language class today so they can do fieldwork?" or "We need to scale back the number of days students are in language classes so the business students can visit more factories." Certainly, there is some flexibility here, but it can be a slippery slope. It is well known that students demonstrate a more dramatic increase in linguistic proficiency if they study the target language before they begin their overseas courses and continue studying the language at the outset of their program abroad (see Brecht et al.), because they are able to take immediate advantage of the foreign language environment.

With respect to short-term summer programs, if well run and truly intensive (small classes meeting for at least four hours each day, carefully integrated community activities, and several hours of daily homework), students can learn as much as in a semester program stateside. However, a summer may be even shorter than it appears, since, just as in semester programs, the schedule must allow some time at the beginning for students to settle in and at the end to prepare for departure. Moreover, when the pace of learning is accelerated, students may end up spending most of their time in the classroom and have little opportunity to explore and interact with the local environment. Make sure you give students what they really want, such as time for independent travel, hands-on opportunities such as internships or service learning, strong interactions with host country citizens, and meaningful ways to improve their language skills. At the same time, you must also give students what they need: strong organization and structure, a well-defined plan for academic study, clear expectations about attendance and active participation, and reasons for undertaking specific study or group travel. If experiential learning is a cornerstone of the program, make sure you schedule adequate time to travel to sites, to undertake laboratory analyses, to work on modeling, etc. In our program, all courses end at 2:10 p.m. each day so that students can use public transportation to get to their labs on the biology campus; travel by bus for fieldwork visits; or head off by bike, bus, or metro to their internships.

Some obvious points are nevertheless worth mentioning: courses taken abroad should count toward major, minor, and degree requirements. Students often shop for study abroad programs seeking the one that will best help them complete these requirements. If your courses count toward an array of academic degrees, more students can benefit, and large enrollments can lead to significant cost savings as expenses are shared across a greater number of participants. Leverage the study abroad environment to design unique courses that cannot be offered on campus, such as the biology modules described earlier. When setting up such courses, it is imperative that you involve faculty members from the departments or academic units whose students you hope to attract. These instructors can advise you as to what sorts of courses abroad best fit their students' educational needs and curricular trajectories.

Getting Started: Choosing Venues

Unless you are integrating the study of a particular discipline into an existing language-based program abroad, you have the opportunity to carefully choose your host country and institution. While Madrid, Florence, or Beijing may sound attractive, other cities can be even more appealing and more helpful toward your objectives. If language acquisition is a primary goal, consider that smaller cities have fewer distractions and often cost substantially less than larger ones (overall program cost is a deciding factor in students' choice of study abroad programs. My advice is to keep it as inexpensive as you can). While it is much easier to recruit for a program in Buenos Aires than for one in Mendoza, Argentina, word of mouth will go a long way toward ensuring future enrollment once a program has been offered successfully. Our choice of Valencia, Spain, was no accident: Iowa students rarely get to spend time near the sea, the city has great historical and cultural attractions, and the university is first-rate. The Mediterranean environment is ideal for both leisure and academic work. Choose a location where you, as program director, will want to return year after year. Whether friends, family, research possibilities, or other connections draw you to the area, selecting a place you love to visit year after year is vital. There is little hope of sustaining a program abroad if you, the person who worked so hard to create the program, no longer wish to spend time there.

Selecting a host institution is as important as choosing a host city and country, and there are many factors to consider beyond the institution's academic or research reputation. For example, private language schools flourish in many countries, and many boast wonderful teachers of language, culture, and literature. Some even offer courses in professions and translation. Private schools often respond much more quickly to program needs than do public universities; but a complex multidisciplinary program usually benefits most from alignment with a large university, which offers more extensive academic resources, facilities, expertise, and personal connections to the local community (e.g., businesses, factories, laboratories, and fieldwork areas). Moreover, with undergraduate research options becoming more and more important, an institution without research expertise may not suit your program. We selected a reputable research university whose highly trained instructors could offer focused course work in many disciplines. We also discovered that, while instructors abroad may not be trained in some of the course work you wish to offer, or may not be accustomed to personally leading fieldwork, they may nevertheless be qualified to teach the courses you are creating and may welcome the opportunity to branch out into new areas and lead foreign students in unique situations.

Whichever institution you choose, make sure there is an office of international education staffed with knowledgeable people who can help with logistics—reserving buses, planning excursions, booking guides, finding professors, reserving space, processing transcripts, etc. Moreover, if experiential learning or undergraduate research (featuring fieldwork, internships, art space, service learning, or the city as a classroom) is a cornerstone of your program, confirm that the institution can accommodate your needs. To attract you, the institution may tell you they can provide everything you need. Do not take such declarations at face value; ensure that there is logistical support, including a very capable main contact person.

Your host institution may offer some of the conveniences that students have come to expect in the United States, such as health and fitness facilities, computer and technology centers, libraries, laboratories, and dining halls. Of course, some universities across the world are unable to provide all of these amenities. Inform students that the lack of such facilities is not indicative of the quality of the institution or the experience. Remind them that they are going abroad to understand how different cultures place emphasis on different things.

Draw on the host professors' strengths or innovations in research and teaching. For example, our students love film, and the University of Valencia has a specialist on post-Franco-dictatorship film. Another faculty member is a specialist on the cultural ramifications of water scarcity. Yet another is a geologist and a leading authority on Mediterranean climate change. These instructors yearn to teach outside their regular courses—and rarely get to do so at their home institution. Note that some universities (or departments) abroad measure prestige by their association with partners from the United States. As a result, turf wars may arise between departments or professors who are vying for those partnerships. Avoid these conflicts at all costs. No matter what side you choose, you will ultimately lose.

Acknowledging Realities and Making Connections with Other Disciplines

While language and literature departments need to promote their own interests in study abroad, it is increasingly important to recognize the other institutional stakeholders in the field, to understand their concerns, and to work with them to ensure a successful experience for students. Language teachers tend to feel that professors outside the humanities do not see the value of what they do. This is a long-standing problem and one that will not find easy resolution in the foreseeable future, particularly amid economic stresses that have prompted the public to question the value of a college degree, the costs of education (language majors tend to be second majors, which can mean a longer term to finish a degree), and the practicality of language study. Language teachers often feel like second-class citizens who must bow to the pressures of colleagues in professional programs. Instead, they should work to advance core goals while integrating the objectives of other disciplines. In other words, professors in different disciplines must work together to formulate and advance the goals of multidisciplinary programs, but I strongly advocate for including language study among them. Language is the entry to culture, and professionals who do not understand another culture will always be at a disadvantage when their competitors do. So, as you embark on developing your program, invite the appropriate stakeholders to the table.

Collaborate with disciplines that belong to essential campus programs or high-priority programs, that attract a lot of students, or that need your expertise in order to create unique international experiences. Look at where your university administration is putting its time and effort (Iowa State emphasizes agriculture, engineering, and STEM areas), because those departments likely receive funding that could also benefit your program. Academic programs with large student populations will automatically give you an audience, thus providing enough participants to satisfy overall budgeting needs and increasing the likelihood that your unique course will be offered. Consider underrepresented majors. Most psychology departments have huge student populations but few study abroad options. The same is true for computer science. How about Developments in Psychology in Vienna, or Japanese Anime in Tokyo?

Once you have targeted a few disciplines that are in need of a study abroad program or are interested in collaborating with you, involve faculty members from those departments in designing unique courses or experiential learning opportunities. If your colleague already has connections at a particular location or university, leverage those relationships. Moreover, enlist as many faculty members from the collaborating departments as you can; those who do not want to direct a program themselves may still offer guidance and help promote your efforts. Seek out complementary experiences, such as opportunities for integrated study, internships, service learning, or undergraduate research that connect to a variety of majors. This will help draw applicants from a diverse group and increase your chances of having enough participants each year to continue the program. I have seen many study abroad initiatives wither due to lack of enrollment. Sustainability has to be a consideration.

Finding the right collaborator can be difficult. As you narrow your list to a few potential colleagues, make sure that you are honest with them from the beginning about the objectives of the program, the expectations for the position, the time commitment and tasks involved, and the positive and negative aspects of the job. It is imperative that all directors be on the same page at all times. Keep in mind that leading a group abroad is a lot more work than teaching at home. Even at universities with a study abroad office, faculty leaders may be charged with many administrative duties such as annual budget management, staff supervision at the host university, negotiation of memoranda of agreement and contracts, emergency and crisis management, excursion and activity planning, and the recruitment and preparation of student participants through information sessions and one-on-one meetings with interested students.[4] On-site directors also deal with a variety of local problems that can be quite demanding. Besides difficulties with faculty members and administrators at the host institution, they must troubleshoot problems as they arise, act as guides, intervene in homestay issues, run interference between students, and help with mundane daily tasks. Students abroad sometimes encounter psychological or medical difficulties, and faculty members must be prepared to assist in getting the necessary help. I often joke that on any given day for the students I function as a father, a psychologist, a police officer, a physician, a tour guide, and sometimes even a teacher! Faculty leaders need to be prepared for these realities, so, in recruiting collaborators, be honest about the upsides *and* the downsides of directing a program abroad. If a colleague is unwilling or unable to perform the required duties, you should look for someone else with whom to collaborate. Most of all, select a colleague whose company you enjoy, because chances are you will spend a great deal of time together at meals, at meetings, and on excursions. If you do not respect your partner, you will definitely have a short collaboration. Communication is crucial, along with the requirement that all students of all disciplines adhere to the same rules. Do not permit students or faculty members to sow division within the program.

Preparing Students: The Before and After

More and more research is demonstrating that orientation and reentry courses are valuable in helping students both prepare for their trip abroad and assimilate their experience upon returning (Cohen et al.). Ensure that students receive predeparture advising to prepare them for the challenging experience of living and studying abroad. We offer six ninety-minute orientation sessions that cover administrative issues, financing study abroad, health and security, Spanish culture and history, living with host families, taking course work at a Spanish university, and many other topics. Our program evaluation results tell us that, although nothing would truly equip students for all potential situations, these orientations help them feel as prepared as possible.

Both before the program and while in the host country, you will need to develop mechanisms for maintaining contact with students. A *Facebook* page, *Twitter* account, or *Blackboard* or *Moodle* page can provide a sense of camaraderie among the students, a go-to place for news and information, and a key avenue of communication.[5]

I also recommend meaningful reentry advising to help students understand their experience abroad and comprehend its impact on their personal and professional lives. My colleagues and I maintain contact with students through informal gatherings, conversations on campus, and *Facebook* or e-mail; in addition, my department offers a one-credit posttravel course that helps students assess what they learned abroad. It requires the enrolled students to give a presentation at a local high school on the value of their study abroad experience. In weekly guest lectures, faculty members, career services personnel, recruiters, and other students counsel participants on how to describe their study abroad experience and related skills in person or on a résumé. I have heard from a number of Fortune 500 recruiters that many job seekers have great difficulty explaining the significance of their experience abroad. Reentry workshops or courses go a long way toward fixing that problem.

Case Study: 2007–16 Statistical Reporting from ISU on the Mediterranean—Summer in Valencia, Spain

Each summer, at the end of our program, we conduct an extensive online evaluation of program quality and management, including predeparture orientations, homestays, excursions, academic course work, and instructors. Students use a five-point Likert scale to rate these elements and to assess their language proficiency and their knowledge of social, cultural, and economic issues in Spain and the European Union. Of the 821 students participating in the program between 2007 and 2016, 534 completed the survey (65.0%). A brief reporting of the results may assist readers in evaluating our program's approach and efficacy. Students have indicated in annual surveys that they are generally quite pleased with the program's structure, organization, and rigor. Between 2007 and 2016, 94.6% of respondents rated the program overall as good or excellent. Two of the chief components of the program—instruction and homestays—received particularly high praise (table 1). We also asked students to assess their understanding of culture abroad and in the United States. Respondents stated that their interest in world events and cultures, their receptivity to different ideas, their tolerance of others, and their self-confidence had all improved or increased as a result of participating in the program (table 2).[6] These are consistent with findings by Vija Mendelson, whose study demonstrated that students who participated in a program abroad experienced profound changes such as "increased independence, self-sufficiency, maturity, and willingness to think with an open mind" (50).[7]

One of the more interesting effects concerns perceptions of language proficiency and cultural awareness: 20.8% of the respondents rated their

Table 1. Program Quality and Management

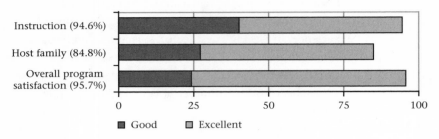

Table 2. Self-Assessment of Cultural Literacy

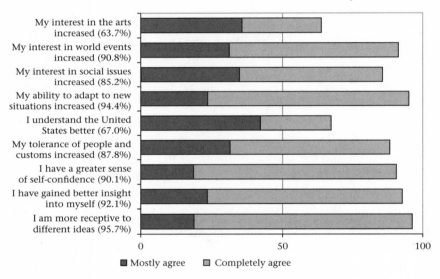

language proficiency as either good or excellent at the beginning of the program. That number increased to 66.2% at the end of the program. Although this proficiency level is self-assessed rather than measured by OPI or ACTFL testing standards, it indicates plainly that students view their abilities in Spanish with greater confidence after completing the program.[8] Such self-assuredness in speaking a second language will help students perform better in class, encourage them to pursue work or further study abroad, and enable them to confidently represent their connection to the host culture. Since many students entered the program with little or no previous training in Spanish, it is not surprising that the immersion environment provided significant gains.[9]

Taken as a whole, our program evaluation statistics suggest that we are meeting many of the objectives we have set for ourselves: students believe we have designed and operated a high-quality program that has increased their global cultural literacy, their self-confidence, and their language proficiency. These are positive, repeatable results from a program that enrolls a large number of students.

Findings and Recommendations

Designing and developing a multidisciplinary program can take years. Making it sustainable takes patience, planning, and dedication on the part of the program directors. Since we founded our program in 2004, we have added new academic components almost every year—which means it has taken thirteen interesting and challenging years to get to where we are today. Along the way, there has been a huge payoff for the directors both personally and professionally as well as for our department. If you can manage to start an interdisciplinary program and make it sustainable, you can achieve the following:

Advanced language and culture training in the target country, even for students who have little interest in learning a second language;

Unique course work and hands-on training that may not be available at the home institution;

Opportunities to work with instructors who have been trained very differently than you and welcome the opportunity to work with foreign colleagues and students;

Higher enrollments in languages: many students continue taking a language upon completion of a program abroad, and some even become majors or minors;

Increased proficiency and comfort in the target language for everyone, including those whose careers will take them abroad;

Increased competency with regard to social, cultural, and political factors, making for better-informed, better-prepared future employees of global companies;

Eyewitness view of difference: a step toward making the world more tolerant and understanding through personal contact with another culture;

Reaffirmation of the viability of language instruction, helping obliterate unfounded claims about English being the only necessary tool for the global marketplace;

Increased visibility of your language, your department, and maybe even your career. Because of the size of our program and the disciplines it cuts across, we have become a model of cross-collaboration at Iowa State University. Indeed, the directors and my Department of World Languages and Cultures are recognized for innovation in language learning and teaching and widely acknowledged as the leaders for internationalization at ISU. Two of us have been given the coveted all-university award for international service. The program itself was a 2015 finalist for the NAFSA Senator Paul Simon Spotlight Award.

Parting Insights

Finally, I offer these guiding principles for the creation of your own program: First, large interdisciplinary programs often involve a great many individual constituents working at different times and at differing paces. Work to treat all students and faculty members across this unwieldy alliance as equally valued participants, and ask that they work for the common good of the program. Next, develop and offer unique courses that allow students ample time to interact with local residents or with their host families, which heightens cultural understanding and appreciation. If you are simply going to put students in a lab abroad for eight hours every day and house them in residence halls, then don't bother going abroad. In other words, don't just mimic what already exists at home. Third, advocate for language and experiential learning as cornerstones of a program abroad, which will provide experiences that cannot be replicated at the home institution. As students gain linguistic and cultural proficiency, those who are not language majors or minors will come to view language learning with greater respect. Similarly, faculty members from other disciplines will likely begin to champion the study of a second language in meetings with students, colleagues, and administrators. Fourth, one great benefit of an interdisciplinary program is the opportunity for different groups to work together and increase mutual appreciation across diverse fields of study. Moreover, there exists an opportunity for faculty members from different disciplines to produce coauthored research, which was one unexpected outcome of my experience. Finally, keep your eye on the bottom line. Students often choose programs based on cost alone, and sharing expenses across a large group can help keep program costs down and student fees attractively low. If you can harness the power of interdisciplinarity abroad, the potential impact on your students, department, and university is great.

NOTES

1. Recent reporting on National Public Radio and *CNNMoney*, and in *The Chronicle of Higher Education*, *The New York Times*, *The New York Post*, *USA Today*, and *The Harvard Business Review*, argues that students with language skills or international experience earn more money, are recruited faster, and are generally more successful in their careers.
2. Julia Domínguez and Leland L'Hote (now program dean for Latin America and Spain at IES Abroad) were my original partners in creating this program. Julia and I were then joined by Cristina Pardo and Julie Wilhelm. Several other colleagues in engineering (David Sly), business (Pol Herrmann, Sekar Raju, and Howard Van Auken), and biology (Steven Rodermel and Beatriz Spalding) have played significant roles as well.
3. Some arguments regarding cultural literacy and business practices have been expressed in other studies I have written ("Cross-Cultural" and "Culture-Based Entrepreneurship Program").
4. Study abroad at Iowa State University is quite decentralized, and individual instructors take on significant leadership, development, and management responsibilities. The university has a study abroad center staffed with several advisers, a director and assistant director, and student ambassadors. The director and assistant director act as advisers for several programs in addition to helping to set policy in conjunction with university attorneys, a risk management office, the university accounting office, and a purchasing department. The business manager at our study abroad center handles billing and collecting student fees, paying overseas providers, and reimbursing program directors. While each college has a study abroad liaison or director who works with students and helps with marketing, policy, and agreements, the vast majority of the work on the program is carried out by the program directors.
5. Many students abroad use free time and digital technologies to blog about their experiences, keep online diaries or photo journals, or make videos. There are, of course, some potential downsides to being so "connected" while abroad, such as not integrating fully into the local culture, ignoring other group members, and being unable to detach from home. My personal view on this subject—from years of observation—is that social media provide helpful ways for students to reflect on their time abroad and come to grips with their daily experience. Online travelogues can also become helpful tools for marketing your program to future students. However, I have noted that the logistical effects of time zones and geography help reduce students' use of these tools. In short, we do not see the numbers of students using *Facebook*, *Twitter*, *Instagram*, *Skype*, or other programs abroad as we do at home. Indeed, although our partner university in Spain is every bit as technologically advanced as our home institution, students tend to veer away from these mediums almost immediately. Anecdotally, students tell me that a combination of factors play a role in that change: on any given day there is much to do and see in the host country; the time difference (seven hours) makes it difficult to use social media in real time with family and friends at home; and they intensely feel part of a new group that they are still getting to know and enjoy. If students are overutilizing these resources, it may say something about the nature of your program or about certain students' personal issues.

6. Similar results regarding cultural sensitivity have been reported by Rob Martinsen. His study included only forty-five participants, and his program was language-based only. Nonetheless, he reports similar findings in improved cultural literacy. I would suggest that because our program is multidisciplinary, with Spanish study being only one of the foci, our results show even greater impact on intercultural competence.

7. Mendelson also showed that students identified the following outcomes as having the greatest impact on their own development: information (learning about study abroad and adapting expectations); integration (acknowledging but avoiding the home culture); interaction (pursuing target language and communication); intention (making a plan and pushing the comfort zone); and introspection (continually reflecting on experiences to put them in perspective) (54).

8. According to Joseph Collentine and Barbara Freed, students abroad did not exhibit more developed grammatical or lexical features than those who stayed in the United States, but they did have greater flexibility in using the language, could produce more sophisticated language, and generally communicated more freely and effectively.

9. Freed summarizes a number of studies that indicate that students with lower language proficiency at the outset of a program make greater gains ("Overview" 44).

Princeton in Cuba: A Study Abroad Program in Havana

Rubén Gallo

Since President Barack Obama announced the reestablishment of diplomatic relations with Cuba on 17 December 2014, Havana has been teeming with American professors, students, researchers, reporters, and cultural agents. Most American study abroad programs were suspended or severely curtailed in the early 2000s, when the second Bush administration tightened restrictions on student travel to Cuba, prohibiting short research trips by undergraduate students. Some of those restrictions were eased after President Obama took office in 2009, and since then several dozen American colleges and universities, including Sarah Lawrence, Brown, Harvard, New York University, Johns Hopkins, and Princeton, have set up study abroad programs in Havana.

All study abroad programs must be sponsored and hosted by a Cuban educational institution. The majority of programs work with the University of Havana, but some have teamed up with literary organizations such as Casa de las Américas, UNEAC (La Union de Escritores y Artistas de Cuba), or the Center for the Study of José Martí. One or two programs also work with ISA (Instituto Superior de Arte), the main art school in Havana.

Most study abroad programs are limited to fifteen students, who travel to Havana accompanied by a resident director, typically a faculty member or, in some cases, an advanced graduate student. Some programs, including Princeton, have both a resident director and a graduate student who assists the director. When the University of Havana is the sponsor, the resident director is expected to attend monthly meetings at the university and must also handle several administrative matters, including paying student registration fees and arranging for the group's health insurance and identification cards. In most other countries these formalities can be completed through the Internet, but in Havana they require in-person visits to banks and government offices.

Until it becomes possible to make bank transfers to the University of Havana, all student registration fees must be paid in cash, in person. When I accompanied a group of students in 2015, I had to withdraw about $10,000 in cash from a local bank and then carry the funds over to a university office (a ten-minute walk), where an employee spent about an hour counting twenty-CUC (convertible peso) bills.

Academics

Most foreign students enroll at the central campus of the University of Havana, located in the Vedado neighborhood—the city's cultural center—where they can take courses in the humanities and social sciences. Typically, students enroll in four or five courses. Among Princeton students, the most popular choices in 2015 were Marxist Leninist Theory, History of the Revolution, Cuban Music, and Afro-Cuban Culture. Some programs also have the resident director teach an introductory course in Cuban history and culture.

From 2015 to 2017, Princeton sent a faculty member to teach two courses for the students participating in the Cuba program. These were considered Princeton courses—they appeared on the university's registrar page—and they had the same reading load and requirements as courses taught on campus. In past years, the Princeton courses have focused on topics such as Cuban literature since the revolution, Havana's urban anthropology, the history of Cuba, and medical anthropology. A third course on Cuban culture was taught by a local professor hired by Princeton. Students then took an additional course or two at the host institution.

The level of instruction at the University of Havana varies greatly according to the professor. Some faculty members are extremely accomplished in their field and have published important books, but their style of teaching—long lectures with no student participation—often jars on American students. Younger professors tend to be more informal and more in sync with the times. The extremely popular course on Marxist Leninism is offered by every department at the university and led by a variety of instructors; in the best cases, it provides American students with an in-depth history of a political and economic model they are unlikely to encounter in their home institutions.

Living Arrangements

There are at least three options for housing students in Havana: first, there are the university dormitories. Foreign students share the same facilities as Cuban students, but Americans usually find the spartan conditions uncomfortable: rooms are small, buildings are often decayed (although the university has recently remodeled one of its main dormitories), meals served are minimal, and there are often water and electricity shortages. A second option, which Princeton used for several years, is a communal house, run privately by a landlord or landlady who rents to foreign college students. Casa Vera is one of the most popular of these houses, a renovated old mansion in Vedado with a small patio and several communal seating areas. There are about twenty double and triple rooms here, housing a total of forty to forty-five students. The landlady charges around $33 per student per day, including breakfast and dinner. The meals are plentiful and delicious, and the rooms provide a level of comfort comparable to that of American dormitories. Such a housing arrangement, however, often means that students end up spending most of their time with other Americans and have limited opportunities to socialize with Cubans or to practice their Spanish. A third option—chosen by Princeton's program in 2016—is to rent several large apartments in a single building and have the landlord cook some meals for the students. The cost is about the same as a communal house, but the students live more independent lives. Four to five students can share a comfortable, fully furnished apartment and can cook some of their own meals, and they have quiet rooms to work in during the day.

Most American study abroad programs house all students in one place. Students from other parts of the world—especially Europeans—often make individual housing arrangements. Since Airbnb began operations in Havana in 2015, it has become easy to rent rooms, apartments, or even houses in Cuba, with the advantage that rent can be paid by credit card using the company's Web site.

Doing Research in Cuba

Students coming from American universities must adapt to the challenges involved in conducting research in Cuba, where government statistics are not easily accessible and certain subjects are considered politically sensitive or outright taboo. Many programs pair American students with a local academic adviser who can help them select an appropriate topic for research. Students of art and literature will have the easiest time: there is a vibrant art world in Havana, and most artists are comfortable speaking English, well versed in American culture, and happy to hold interviews and studio visits with foreign students. The same goes for literature scholars, who will have access to local writers and poets.

History majors will have some difficulty finding books and articles, except for material published in Cuba by state-owned publishers; students of politics will face the most restrictions and will be discouraged from working on a number of topics or subjects that are considered sensitive. The same goes for those interested in medical anthropology, or for students of sociology working on issues such as poverty, gentrification, or class mobility. Material on all of these issues will be difficult to find in Cuba. Some successful independent research projects undertaken by Princeton students in recent years include "Recent Trends in Performance Art," "A Study of the Use of Public Space in City Parks," "Interviews with Musicians," "A Study of New Restaurants and Bars," and "El paquete semanal" (often called the "Cuban Internet").

Students doing their own research will find conducting interviews easy as long as they avoid government institutions, including hospitals and government offices. Most state employees will balk at the prospect of being interviewed by American students. Entrepreneurs, on the other hand, are for the most part willing to grant informal interviews to students. Since the entrepreneurial class is the newest and fastest-growing sector in the Cuban economy, students will have access to an exciting field of research by meeting with owners of bars, restaurants, and rental properties, and even with CD and DVD vendors.

Urban anthropology, broadly defined, is also a fertile field for student research. Havana is a dynamic city, full of contradictions, and students have written research papers on topics including the rise of subcultures such as emos and punks; the uses of streets, parks, and other public space; and the role of religion in Cuban life.

Curriculum

In early 2015, I spent a semester teaching a group of ten Princeton students in Havana. I was accompanied by a graduate student who also served as resident director and as the main liaison with the university. Princeton rented office space in Havana—an apartment in Vedado—which we used to hold our classes and meetings. One advantage of having a meeting space of this kind is that students feel freer to express themselves and to ask questions that might be considered uncomfortable in an official space such as the University of Havana.

Havana: Urban Anthropology was a course designed to send students out into the streets, inviting them to analyze different aspects of life in Havana's public spaces. As a textbook, we used *Havana beyond the Ruins: Cultural Mappings after 1989*, a collection of essays and articles edited by Anke Birkenmaier and Esther Whitfield. This excellent anthology brings together writers and cultural critics who explore aspects of everyday life in Havana, including the proliferation of vernacular and self-built architecture, the rise of independent restaurants—the first sector of the Cuban economy to be liberalized in the 1990s—and the cultural meanings of popular music.

Early in the semester, students were asked to select a site anywhere in Havana to study throughout the course, which would serve as a case study of contemporary life in Cuba. The class was run as a workshop, and each week one of the students would make an in-class presentation, frequently illustrated with *PowerPoint*, about his or her site. Other students would then suggest ways to think about that particular space in the context of the Cuban transition. This course required weekly one-page papers—field notes or an analysis of the site from a specific angle—in addition to a final fifteen-page research paper presenting the semester-long research in a polished form, including a critical bibliography.

Havana: Urban Anthropology was a great success: students loved the opportunity to explore Havana on their own and to think about urban space with critical rigor. One student chose to work on the orthodox synagogue in Old Havana and then expanded her research to include the history of Cuba's Jewish community; another student studied the basilica at Regla, a Catholic church frequented by parishioners who also practice Afro-Cuban religions, and used the opportunity to interview both the resident priest and the various *santeros*—Afro-Cuban practitioners—who work in the park facing the church. Other research projects focused on Santeria stores, a park frequented by goth teenagers, a ruined sports park, and a park in Old Havana where tourists cross paths with sex workers.

The second course, Cuban Literature after the Revolution, examined intersections of culture and politics after 1959. We read examples of early revolutionary enthusiasm—Che Guevara's theories of socialism and a selection of Fidel Castro's speeches—followed by chronicles of gradual disillusionment by writers who chose exile, such as Guillermo Cabrera Infante. A section of the course focused on the persecution of gay writers in the 1960s, as chronicled by Reinaldo Arenas in his autobiography, *Antes que anochezca* (*Before Night Falls*). We spent two weeks on 1971—the darkest year of what has been called "the gray five-year period" ("quinquenio gris"; Fornet 379)— and discussed the case of Heberto Padilla, a poet who was imprisoned and forced to offer a public apology for having published a poetry collection that was deemed counterrevolutionary.

Upon arriving in Cuba, students hear much about the "special period," as Cubans refer to the decade of the 1990s. These years following the collapse of the Soviet Union—and the end of the Soviets' $6 billion annual subsidies to the island—were marked by severe food and fuel shortages. One of the best chronicles of this period is Pedro Juan Gutiérrez's *Dirty Havana Trilogy*, a collection of stories focusing on poor characters in Centro Habana.

The final weeks of the course focused on writers active today: Wendy Guerra, a woman novelist who writes about her childhood in *Everyone Leaves*; Leonardo Padura, who has risen to international acclaim with his detective novels; and the new generation of bloggers and performance poets.

Practical Information

Visas

Student and faculty visas are processed at the Cuban embassy in Washington, DC. The process has become much smoother now that the embassy can accept money orders (in the past all payments had to be made in person and in cash). Visas must be coordinated by the American institution and the Cuban host organization, and take about eight weeks to process.

Health

Cuba has a first-rate medical system. American students must purchase insurance through Asistur, a Cuban company, which gives them access to the Cira García Hospital, one of the best in Havana. The most common ailments experienced by American students are minor gastrointestinal infections that can be treated with a simple course of antibiotics.

Money

As of September 2018, American credit and debit cards do not work in Cuba. Students must travel with enough cash for the semester (most programs recommend $500 per month). Money can also be wired though Western Union, but the process is slow, expensive, and complicated. Students with access to cards issued by a bank outside the United States (such as a European, Canadian, or Latin American bank) can withdraw funds at banks and ATMs in Havana and other major cities.

Most resident directors use a service provided by various foreign companies to receive funds from their home institution. Funds must be wired to a third country, like Mexico or Canada, deposited in a special account, and then withdrawn in Cuba using an ATM card provided by the company. The fees for using this service—including exchange fees and commissions—range from fifteen to twenty percent.

Emerging Issues in Study Abroad

Sarita Rai

Study abroad is not a singular discipline. Rather, it cuts across multiple disciplines such as foreign languages, arts and humanities, the sciences, history, and political science. Thus, study abroad does not belong only to those professionals who work in the area of international education; its policies and programs reflect departments' curricular changes, students' interests and activities, and institutions' traditions and dynamics, as well as the interactions of many stakeholders.

This essay looks at some emerging issues affecting both the present and the future of study abroad. Rather than trace the history of each one, I will examine their influence today and suggest ways to anticipate their development in the future. Topics include student access to study abroad programs; the differences between exchange programs and study abroad; the impact on study abroad of the globalization and financialization of universities; the implications of the locus of study abroad within the organizational structure of the university; and safety and security. All of these issues are multifaceted, affected by changes in institutions' missions and goals concerning everything from student retention to administrative priorities. Keeping this in mind, I hope to outline and clarify the challenges that administrators, professors, and students are likely to encounter in the coming decades.

Student Access to Study Abroad Programs

Access is generally understood as the quality of being approachable and reachable. It suggests ease of movement toward entry and the ability to cross a perceived threshold or actual doorway. In order to facilitate access, personnel in study abroad must make their presence well known on campus and help navigate the obstacles that the students believe may prevent them from studying overseas.

Relevant Messaging

Perhaps the most basic way to get students past the threshold that separates on-campus and off-campus study is to speak to, and with, them. Speaking takes many forms, from conversations and classroom visits to video presentations to Web site descriptions and design. The text on the Web site should be welcoming to all students, especially those who statistically are underrepresented in overseas study. We all know that research by international education specialists has become increasingly data-driven. The publications are sophisticated, analyzing the importance of intercultural competencies, global student mobility, internationalization, and globalization. Publications that are embedded with data may justify and legitimize the field of international education, but they do not necessarily make a case for reaching out and speaking to students. As Mark Salisbury argues in "We're Muddying the Message on Study Abroad" in *The Chronicle of Higher Education*, an emerging study abroad issue is the need "to disentangle the rhetoric from the reality."

Promises of abstract benefits such as cross-cultural learning, improved critical thinking, increased empathy, global citizenry, and future job offers may not be highly effective as an initial exposure to study abroad. Students looking casually at a Web site or a brochure are unlikely to respond to what Salisbury calls "lofty" language. Michael Woolf warns against exaggeration in promotional language "to the point where unrealistic expectations are established and where the rhetoric is burdened by hyperbole," since such "rhetoric masks and distorts tangible benefits that are far from being elusive" (47). Relevant messaging depends on appropriate communication and a commitment to designing accessible programs. If marketing messages are appealing and relevant to students, they may actually succeed.

Underrepresented Students

Salisbury warns against a "one-size-fits-all" approach. He offers the example of a minority student who already may be in a new environment with new pressures and expectations to meet. The student may feel little incentive to travel thousands of miles to experience even greater unfamiliarity under the rubric of global relations. Study abroad officers who hope to diversify participation need to engage with the priorities and concerns of the population on campus—including racial minorities, the LGBTQ community, first-generation college-bound and low-income students, to name a few—and provide support throughout the study abroad sojourn. Support may take the forms of ensuring the availability of financial aid on campus and helping with the necessary paperwork; creating a culture of inclusivity and multiculturalism; clearly explaining expectations and evaluation systems in the classroom; cross-cultural training; and predeparture and postreturn programming during and after the study abroad experience. In other words, successful directors must be able to conceive of new modes of support for a changing student profile.

Salisbury does not argue for an elementary simplicity. He does argue, though, for shaping messages that clearly describe intentional learning goals under specific parameters. He wants study abroad personnel to implement or revise systems that will strengthen both recruitment and retention, making programs abroad more feasible for minority groups. The task of reducing barriers will continue to be a goal for those involved in study abroad.

Financial Aid

Financing one's education is not a new problem but one that is becoming more and more critical. Funding for higher education has been cut severely while the expense of attendance at private and public schools has skyrocketed. Stories of enormous student debt are often in the news. Writing in *Forbes*, Zack Friedman places student loan debt into "the second highest consumer debt category—behind only mortgage debt—and higher than both credit cards and auto loans." The details are staggering: "There are more than 44 million borrowers with $1.3 trillion in student loan debt in the U.S. alone. The average student in the Class of 2016 has $37,172 in student loan debt." Although the larger underlying phenomenon is, in good part, generated by the financialization of higher education, each individual caught in the web of that process must work mightily to meet debt obligations. Charlie Eaton, a sociologist at the University of California, Berkeley, warns that the commodifying and financializing of the economy, which includes higher education, is indeed dangerous. Increased "reliance on financial investment returns and increasing costs from transactions to acquire capital" are linked to an increase in student debt and in borrowing by colleges and universities that cannot afford it (Eaton, "Financialization"). As Eaton demonstrates, the excess interest payments on debt on a per-student basis and very large endowment assets at some of our wealthiest schools have put unprecedented pressure on higher education.

Financial aid will always be part of the picture of study abroad even as the picture looks more and more complicated by economic factors and large-scale funding ventures. Directors of study abroad will need to be both diligent and ethically responsible in pricing their programs. Ideally, study abroad should be affordable to all segments of the university population. If study abroad is viewed less as an educational opportunity than as a venue expected to show profits, quality may be sacrificed. Some schools may withhold federal and state money from study abroad in order to keep those funds on the home campus. Of course, education is not free, but, at a time when outside funding is in a steep decline, directors will have to be judicious mediators, finding ways to maintain quality offerings without creating arguments with other offices of the institution. Clearly, directors will have to think very seriously about the priorities they have established for their programs. It is reasonable to assume that students attending study abroad programs should pay approximately what they would normally pay while attending their home institution. However, it is also important that study abroad not be prohibitively expensive. Programs in India or Botswana or even countries in Europe may cost less than in-state tuition per semester at a public institution. Thoughtful costing of programs can increase access for financially needy students.

All institutions of higher education, regardless of their public or private status, are legally required to let students who receive federal and institutional financial student aid use the funds to pay for their time abroad. These forms of aid include Pell grants, subsidized loans, and unsubsidized loans. Additionally, any federally funded research grants will most likely have a component to enable graduate or undergraduate students to study abroad.

Such grants awarded through the National Science Foundation, the Department of Education, the National Institute of Health, and the Department of Agriculture, for example, require that the principal investigator include a study abroad segment. While federal research grant funding and scholarships can be a great impetus to energize participation in study abroad, these are not sustaining sources of funding for students.

Much has been written about schools that want institutional financial aid funding to stay on campus rather than get spent abroad. Securing adequate funding for education abroad ought not to be a problem—apart from the national problem of guaranteeing equal access for all students to all of American higher education. The most important duty of the education-abroad administrator is to make studying abroad a viable alternative. Through knowledge, communication, and networking, regular and alternative sources of financial aid can be found. "The time involved may seem daunting, but the rewards to students make the effort worthwhile" (Stubbs 48).

Access for Students with Disabilities

Access also means access to study abroad programs for students who are disabled. Section 504 of the Rehabilitation Act and Titles II and III of the Americans with Disabilities Act (ADA) define a person with disability as one who has "a physical or mental impairment that substantially limits one or more major life activities," who has "a history or record of such an impairment," or who "is perceived by others as having such an impairment." Section 504 adds, "Higher education institutions must also consider whether the individual is otherwise qualified, *i.e.* 'able to carry out the essential requirements of the [study abroad] program with or without reasonable accommodation'" (United States). Attention to these legal definitions is very important; compliance is federally mandated.

Evidence of compliance with the law can readily be found on campuses throughout the United States. Offices such as the Kokua Program at the University of Hawai'i at Mānoa (www.hawaii.edu/kokua/) are dedicated to the service of students with disabilities. Faculty members generally know that students with a documented disability have access to a range of accommodations in their on-campus classes—note takers, extra testing time, sign language interpreters, and so on—and it is customary now to include information on a course syllabus concerning accommodations for students with disabilities. Considerable literature on disability in study abroad is available. The Web site of the Office for Equity and Diversity at the University of Minnesota, for instance, provides a list of accommodations for conditions such as attention deficit hyperactivity disorder, autism spectrum disorder, hearing problems, and more (diversity.umn.edu/disability/home).

Strides have been made in these areas, but the literature also shows that compliance can be challenging when it involves individuals who cross international borders, as is the case in study abroad. Every situation is different and requires individual attention. The study abroad director should consult the disabilities office on campus to learn whether a student can meet the essential program requirements with or without reasonable accommodation. It is often possible to find ways to reasonably accommodate a student's special needs. However, if providing accommodations means that the nature of the programming goals will be compromised, the ADA requirement abroad will not be of paramount concern. For instance, a program in London, whose personnel have experience in accommodating many students with disabilities, might have a housing coordinator, an adequate number of advisers, and ways of providing access to classes. If, however, a program is based in a rural mountainous agricultural setting of a developing country for the primary learning outcome of understanding how diseases transfer from animals to people, accommodation could be extremely difficult to arrange. The desired outcome might depend essentially on being in the farmers' living quarters and collecting microbes. It would be difficult for a wheelchair-bound student who also needs personal care to participate fully in this particular program without essential changes to course content and objectives. Asking individual farmers to change their living quarters, or limiting the student's participation in site visits and activities, would alter the nature and experience of the program. Heidi Soneson advocates a thorough exploration of available options:

> Some overseas staff may be quite open to the request and may have provided accommodations in the past. Many overseas contacts may not have considered disability accommodations previously or may feel overwhelmed by the thought of making accommodations for an individual student. In these cases, the host culture may not typically offer special services to individuals with disabilities or consider the range of disabilities accepted in the United States as needing special accommodations. . . . As a result, it is essential

to encourage students to [voluntarily] disclose as early as possible so that there is sufficient time to explore options with the overseas site.   (10)

Study abroad directors have to keep up with case law concerned with disabilities. An especially thorny question is whether ADA applies to offshore programs. Many other questions follow: How much authority does a university in the United States have over the foreign institution its students attend? How can the university ensure students' safety if the program is in a country that does not have disability laws and protections in any way comparable to our own? How should the university encourage students to disclose their disability to ensure enough time for all options to be explored?

Disability laws are certain to be a key issue in higher education in the coming years. Though some programs may not be appropriate for everyone, others are, and study abroad personnel should be thoroughly trained in order to advise wisely and instill confidence in the inquiring student. Participating teachers will also need to be aware of the ADA laws that require certain types of accommodations.

Exchange Programs versus Study Abroad Programs

One way to think about these differently designed programs is to consider exchange as a two-way plan; students temporarily exchange places at their respective schools. Study abroad programs are one-way plans, and reciprocity does not come into play. Each program has advantages and disadvantages for both the students and the institutions. The study abroad director who is committed to good advising will inform students of the full range of overseas opportunities. When appropriate, students should be encouraged to speak with advisers in international exchange (if study abroad and exchange are separated into different offices). Both types of programs certainly broaden students' academic and social experiences. Both foster cooperation between the participating institutions, and both help to diversify the respective student populations.

Exchange programs come about through bilateral agreements between universities. From an institutional standpoint, these agreements confer a certain amount of prestige, for they give evidence of an international educational reach. In theory, the partner institutions serve the same number of exchange students, who cross the globe in reciprocal fashion. Again theoretically, there need not be an exchange of tuition money because each school accepts the same number of students. Exchange students attend classes that are already offered within the regular curricula; no courses are designed for the visiting students, who register for what seems to best suit them.

Exchange programs are geared to students who want considerable independence: there is generally no resident director to organize excursions, to serve as a resource, or to teach a class, and students are responsible for their own housing, meals, and all costs associated with living and studying abroad. Students registering for the exchange option must also understand that classes will be in the language of the country. Most foreign students who attend an American college on exchange have previously studied English and are proficient in English. They are able to pass the TOEFL, IELTS, or most other tests of English language requirements. Typically, acquiring foreign language proficiency is less important to American students (excluding language majors). As a consequence, many are confined to exchange programs in regions where classes are taught in English.

Reciprocal partnerships will surely continue as globalization and internationalism are emphasized in higher education. For students in the United States, this means having a wide array of participating schools from which to choose. It also means having considerable freedom as well as personal and academic responsibility, from ensuring that credits will transfer over to the home institution to independently planning and paying for excursions. Program directors on home campuses in the United States must ensure that students grasp the differences and similarities between exchange programs and study abroad. Students may have a hard time sifting through the relative benefits, requirements, and costs of the programs, especially if there are separate directors and separate offices. Both offices should distinguish the defining characteristics of their programs on their Web sites and in their promotional materials and presentations. Despite the complexities introduced by variations in student participation, semester length, staff responsibilities, and revenues, exchange programs and study abroad programs are not mutually exclusive and can help to sustain each other.

Globalization and Financialization

The first paragraph of this essay makes the point that study abroad reflects the values of an institution and the interests of its students, faculty members, and administrators. In turn, the university reflects and responds to larger cultural, economic, and political trends, which, in our century, have been globalization and financialization. Much has been written on the impact of these two phenomena, and certainly most if not all study abroad personnel are thoroughly informed and knowledgeable. Globalization refers to a worldview and a world market that involve the mobility of people, goods, ideas, and services. Aided by technology, globalization fosters interdependent curricula and initiatives. These are communicated and shared, and eventually they may become part of an extensive or global network. In terms immediately relevant to this essay, globalization can draw greater attention to the policies and values of study abroad. It may be easier for teachers to experiment with new approaches and activities off campus rather than on campus, especially when a class includes international students as well as students coming from the United States. Participants from multiple locations, and the relative absence of home-campus bureaucracy, may foster openness and innovation.

One role of study abroad is to encourage participating professors to introduce methodologies and content that foster a sense of the global. Tact may be necessary if the director, in addition to administration, must watch over academic integrity without heavy-handed monitoring of participating instructors. Professors may adopt new modes of cross-border teaching involving experiential learning as well as online deliveries; or they can propose internationally partnered teaching and innovative grading criteria. Indeed, study abroad can be a leader in facilitating programs such as one at the University of North Carolina, where students spend two to four semesters at the National University of Singapore and graduate with degrees from both schools. The school of architecture at the University of Hawai'i, which offers a dual doctoral degree in architecture with Tongji University in Shanghai, sends professors abroad to teach and to develop academic and business ties. Such creative uses of the host location and local environment arise from global awareness and a thoughtful world view.

Financialization has been less beneficial for study abroad. It's no secret that public and nonprofit universities have been pulled toward the marketplace more than ever before. Staff members of study abroad may well be urged to charge more for some programs than is absolutely necessary. Indeed, the pressures to view a program as a profitable venture are widespread. It's impossible to ignore shrinking budgets and state and federal funding cuts, but the advent of financialization in the early twenty-first century has led to serious fiduciary problems for many colleges. Mike Konczal defines financialization as the "increase in size, scope and power of the financial sector—the people and firms that manage money and underwrite stocks, bonds, derivatives, and other securities—relative to the rest of the economy" (qtd. in Eaton, "Financialization"). Konczal has much to say on the consequences of financialization for higher education. The pressure to compete and the high stakes involved have been instrumental in mingling education and finance: "increases in overall borrowing by colleges and universities, increases in the cost of interest payments on debt on a per-student basis, and a concentration of endowment assets at a small group of the wealthiest institutions—[is] a form of concentration of wealth." He concludes that financialization has harmed higher education because it has "increased social and economic inequalities, instead of serving as the equal-izer we have long imagined college to be" (qtd. in Russel 4). The statement criticizes public and nonprofit institutions that have been pulled toward the marketplace and driven by capital and pressure to maximize profits.

A 2013 study entitled "Bankers in the Ivory Tower" found that from 2005 to 2011 the University of California more than doubled its outstanding bond debt. The funds went to medical centers, dormitories, and athletic facilities (which heighten the school's profile in very visible ways) while basic academic services decreased. The authors of the study use this situation to illustrate how the "financialization of university governance" has reoriented education "towards financial strategies and financial markets" (Eaton, "Bankers" 3). They attribute this change to the hiring of managers of finance and individuals with Wall Street experience to join the administration and the university's board of regents. The finances of schools differ according to circumstances, but the large amount of debt accumulated by university administrations in order to build facilities such as athletics complexes, dormitories, and campus malls with shopping centers is well known.

Study abroad officials must diligently protect their office's budgets and those of their students. Ethical as well as financial responsibility demands that no student be encouraged to accrue excessive debt for studying abroad. Financial pressures affect academic matters and ultimately influence program funding, expansion, and sustainability. It is probably safe to say that globalization and financialization will continue to bring both predictable and unforeseen changes to higher education. Knowledge and technology will continue to cross borders and to bring regions and nations into ever-increasing contact, cooperation, and competition.

Location of Study Abroad

The location of study abroad within the administrative structure of a university is an indication of how its purpose is understood. In accordance with the history and development of the institution, the office will likely operate under the aegis of student services or academic affairs. Students should receive good counseling wherever the office is placed, so it behooves study abroad personnel to be knowledgeable about both departments and to work within the limits of what they understand will be feasible.

Study abroad under the aegis of student services tends to provide individual support services. In their essay "The Education-Abroad Office in Its Campus Context," Paul DeYoung and Paul Primak note that study abroad personnel "may be limited to general advising and travel services, seldom becoming involved with program development, recruitment and selection, or academic credit" (19). The drawbacks of this model have to be considered. Students may leave their home school without assurances of mentoring or on-site academic advising. Home institution faculty members do not necessarily accompany the students overseas. The home and host institution do not always work as close partners, and office staff members have little jurisdiction over whether credits earned abroad will be transferable to the home department.

Study abroad offices within the department of academic affairs tend to focus on the academic elements of the overseas experience. Faculty members may serve as resident directors who accompany students abroad and teach at the host institution, usually courses relevant to the site. Students can feel secure about course credits, since courses in such programs typically have home-institution equivalents.

Neither location is intrinsically better, and many variations exist as institutions age and alter their organizational structures, adding positions and consolidating others. Study abroad directors need to understand their school's structure and their role within it. Because study abroad involves so many different offices, changes occur slowly. What do the academic departments want? Do individual professors seek advice on conducting their courses abroad? What do the larger divisions believe is important? What information is being reported by the financial aid office? Do the departmental chairs and school administrators support the director's efforts? Perhaps most important, what do staff members hear from students—those who decide to go abroad and those who don't? All this is to say that campus visibility and maintaining good will are both crucial factors in the success of your programs.

Safety and Security

Student safety is the most fundamental priority of study abroad. Some problems can be averted by risk management orientations, which are a mainstay of most programs. The center at the University of Hawai'i mandates that all students and faculty members participating in study abroad for any length of time attend twelve hours of predeparture cross-cultural and risk management training. These sessions are both comprehensive and detailed, presenting a wide range of contingencies, scenarios, and appropriate responses. The risk management segment teaches students and faculty members how to manage and document accidents and how to contact study abroad personnel (twenty-four hours a day), notes which local resources are immediate responders, explains elements of cross-cultural safety, and lays out emergency procedures. Students and faculty members learn whom to text, call, and e-mail at the host school, in the town, and, if necessary, at the American consulate. They can identify their first line of support and grasp the crucial importance of letting their families and the university know their whereabouts. From there, the study abroad center can contact others at home and abroad to make any arrangements that might be necessary.

Paul Glye, in "Study Abroad in a Time of Terror: U.S. Student Experiences in Brussels," confirms the importance of the procedures above. Glye and seventeen students were in Brussels in March 2016 when the airport and a metro station were attacked. They were all unharmed, but, as *The New York Times* reported, "the bombings paralyzed Brussels, . . . prompted international travel warnings to avoid Belgium, and reverberated across the Atlantic to the United States, where New York and other major cities raised terrorism threat levels" (qtd. in Glye 15). Glye followed his protocols, keeping his students calm and ascertaining that everyone had communicated with their families. He also made contact with his partner school in Brussels and his home institution. Two days after the event, Glye asked his students to write down their thoughts from the day of the attack and their subsequent reflections. Most of his article presents students' emotional responses and resolve to continue in their program. Students described feeling "sudden bonds" with the local community. They found themselves "to be part of a sudden emotional fabric that they could not have imagined the day before" (21).

There are lessons here for all involved in study abroad. Directors and members of their staff should emphasize to prospective students what safety measures are in place and reiterate them throughout the pre-departure meetings. There are definite advantages to having a faculty resident director whom students can turn to in emergency situations. Although violence unfortunately occurs across the globe, we can say that studying abroad will continue to be valuable, and that universities will focus on refining their safety measures and policies to meet unknown contingencies. As Gyles's students make clear, studying abroad, even in the midst of the most difficult of situations, remains a vital element in their lives.

NOTES ON CONTRIBUTORS

MONIQUE CHYBA is professor of mathematics at the University of Hawai'i at Mānoa. Her contributions range from robotics, especially optimal guidance and navigation of autonomous underwater vehicles, to applications in the medical field. She is coeditor of *Recent Advances in Celestial and Space Mechanics* (2016), *Singular Trajectories and their Role in Control Theory* (2003), and more than seventy peer-reviewed journal and conference papers. She has received the Science and Lectureship Award from Chiba University and the Regents' Medal for Excellence in Teaching from the University of Hawai'i. Active in outreach, she has developed an educational afternoon program for the Institute for Human Services on Oahu.

TANIA CONVERTINI is research assistant professor in the Department of French and Italian at Dartmouth College, where she directs the language program. She specializes in language and language pedagogy, digital pedagogy, the use of cinema and literature in language teaching, Italian cinema, and Italian literature of the twentieth and twenty-first centuries. She has published articles on language learning, Italian literature and film, and the use of technology in the language classroom, and is currently working on a media studies project on the Italian humanist and educator Alberto Manzi.

ROSANNE FLESZAR DENHARD is professor of English at Massachusetts College of Liberal Arts. Her interests encompass early modern British literature and interdisciplinary studies, literature in performance, life writing, early modern women, and pedagogy. She teaches a wide range of courses, including Shakespeare, Medieval and Early Modern English Drama, Life-Writing Senior Seminar, Milton, and the Arts of Medieval and Renaissance Britain travel course. She prioritizes pedagogy and mentoring and serves on the Undergraduate Research Council and Honors Advisory Board at MCLA. Her honors include the MCLA Faculty Association Senior Faculty Award for outstanding teaching and service and the Senior Class Faculty Appreciation Award for teaching and mentoring.

MIRIAM FUCHS is professor of English and vice president of the Center for Biographical Research at the University of Hawai'i. She is the author of *The Text Is Myself: Women's Life Writing and Catastrophe* (Wisconsin UP) and coeditor with Craig Howes of *Teaching Life Writing Texts* (MLA). She has published *Marguerite Young, Our Darling: Tributes and Essays* (Dalkey), coedited with Ellen G. Friedman *Breaking the Sequence: Women's Experimental Fiction* (Princeton UP), and guest edited issues of *Biography: An Interdisciplinary Quarterly* and *Review of Contemporary Fiction*. An author in the Princeton Legacy Library, she has published articles on modernism, Djuna Barnes, Emily Holmes Coleman, T. S. Eliot, H.D., Patricia Grace, and the diaries and autobiography of Hawai'i's Queen Lili'uokalani. She has received numerous teaching awards from the University of Hawai'i including the Regents' Medal for Excellence in Teaching.

RUBÉN GALLO is Walter S. Carpenter Jr. Professor in Language, Literature and Civilization of Spain at Princeton University. He is the author of *Proust's Latin Americans* (2014), *Freud's Mexico: Into the Wilds of Psychoanalysis* (2010), *Mexican Modernity: The Avant-Garde and the Technological Revolution* (2005), *New Tendencies in Mexican Art* (2004), and *The Mexico City Reader* (2004). He received the Gradiva award for the best book on a psychoanalytic theme and the Modern Language Association's Katherine Singer Kovacs Prize for the best book on a Latin American topic. He is currently at work on *Cuba: A New Era*, about the changes in Cuban culture after the diplomatic thaw with the United States.

CHAD M. GASTA is professor of Spanish and chair of the Department of World Languages and Cultures at Iowa State University, where he directs programs in international studies and codirects the Languages and Cultures for Professions program. He teaches courses on contemporary Spain and Spanish for business and the professions as well as courses on the literatures and cultures of early modern Spain and Latin America. He is the author of *Imperial Stagings: Empire and Ideology in Transatlantic Theater of Early Modern Spain and The New World* (2013), *Transatlantic Arias: Early Opera in Spain and the New World* (2013), and an annotated critical edition of *Lazarillo de Tormes* (2013).

CELESTE KINGINGER is professor of applied linguistics at Pennsylvania State University, where she teaches courses in second language acquisition and education as well as advanced seminars such as Narrative Approaches to Multilingual Identity, Second Language Pragmatics, and Approaches to Language in Use. She is affiliated with the Center for Advanced Language Proficiency Education and Research, funded by the United States Department of Education, and with the Center for Language Acquisition in the university's College of Liberal Arts. Her research has examined telecollaborative, intercultural language learning; second language pragmatics; cross-cultural life writing; teacher education; and study abroad.

L I J I N is associate professor in the Department of Modern Languages at DePaul University in Chicago. She directs the Chinese studies program and created the university's summer intensive language program in Shanghai. She obtained her PhD in second language acquisition and instructional technology at University of South Florida. Her research interests include technology-enhanced second-language teaching and learning, study abroad, Chinese pragmatics learning, identity (re-)configuration, sociocultural theory and ecology in language education, and intercultural learning.

Y V E S L O I S E A U is pedagogical director of the Centre International d'Études Françaises at Université Catholique de l'Ouest in Angers, France. He specializes in language pedagogy for graduate students studying to be French language teachers of international students. After receiving his doctorate from the Université de Paris 3 Sorbonne Nouvelle, he taught at the University of Sanaa in Yemen; the University of Kumasi in Ghana; and the National University of Panama. He is an active researcher in language education and technology and specializes in *formation didactique*—pedagogy for large groups. He has published many pedagogical guides and texts as well as theoretical investigations in all areas of language teaching.

M I N D I M C M A N N is associate professor of English at the College of New Jersey. Her teaching and research interests are in postcolonial and anglophone literature, intersections of literature and political philosophy, and critical race studies. Her work focuses on contemporary South African, Irish, British, and Nigerian literature. She has published in *MFS: Modern Fiction Studies*, *Paradoxa*, and *College Literature*.

J O A N N P H I L L I O N is professor of curriculum studies at Purdue University, where she teaches graduate courses in curriculum and multicultural education and an undergraduate course in preservice teacher education. Specializing in social justice issues, she has published extensively on her research in an inner-city Canadian school and has conducted research on minority students in Hong Kong and preservice teachers' understanding of diversity. Her publications include *Narrative Inquiry in a Multicultural Landscape: Multicultural Teaching and Learning* (2002); *Narrative and Experience in Multicultural Education* (2005) as coeditor; the *Handbook of Curriculum and Instruction* (2008); *Minority Students in East Asia* (2011); and *Internationalizing Teacher Education for Social Justice: Research, Theory and Practice* (2014).

SARITA RAI, professor and director of study abroad for the University of Hawai'i at Mānoa, is in charge of twenty-seven international programs. She has a PhD in political science and is a trained political economist as well as a language specialist in Nepalese. Her interests lie in the areas of globalization, global studies, shared governance, and faculty governance. She is active in leadership positions in the University of Hawai'i Faculty Senate and the Professional Assembly, which is the faculty union organization. She has been a Fulbright scholar in India.

SUNITI SHARMA is associate professor in the Department of Teacher Education at Saint Joseph's University, Philadelphia. She teaches ESL pedagogy, instructional techniques for social studies, and English language arts and assessment and evaluation. Her research focuses on multicultural competencies for preservice teachers and the education of at-risk youth. She is the author of *Girls Behind Bars: Reclaiming Education in Transformative Spaces* (2013) and has coedited *Internationalizing Teacher Education for Social Justice: Theory, Research and Practice* (2014) and published in peer-reviewed journals such as *Teachers College Record*, *Race Ethnicity and Education*, and *Frontiers: The Interdisciplinary Journal of Study Abroad*.

JOSÉ ANTONIO TORRALBA is a senior investigator at the Open University of Catalonia (Department of Food Systems, Culture and Society), where he leads the Food Profile, a project that designs school-based curricula based on research into the daily eating practices of school-age children and youth in Spain and Denmark. He also coleads a Europe-wide Erasmus+ project aimed at promoting better health among students through a set of evidence-based initiatives. His research interests are in the learning processes of children in and out of schools, the design of learning and teaching environments, factors associated with access to education among minority groups and immigrants, and service learning.

WORKS CITED

ADFL Executive Committee. "Best Practices in Study Abroad: A Primer for Chairs of Departments of Foreign Languages." *ADE Bulletin*, nos. 147–48, Winter-Spring 2009, pp. 72–76.

Agar, Michael. *Language Shock: Understanding the Culture of Conversation*. William Morrow, 1994.

Ai Weiwei: Never Sorry. Directed by Alison Klayman, produced by Klayman and Adam Schlesinger, 2012.

Aljaafreh, Ali, and James P. Lantolf. "Negative Feedback as Regulation and Second Language Learning in the Zone of Proximal Development." *Modern Language Journal*, vol. 78, no. 4, 1994, pp. 465–83.

Arenas, Reinaldo. *Before Night Falls*. Translated by Dolores M. Koch, Penguin, 1994.

Arianrhod, Robyn. *Einstein's Heroes: Imagining the World through the Language of Mathematics*. Oxford UP, 2013.

Association of Departments of Foreign Languages. "Best Practices in Study Abroad: A Primer for Chairs of Departments of Foreign Languages." *ADFL Bulletin*, vol. 40, nos. 2-3, Winter-Spring 2009, pp. 72–76.

Atalay, Bulent. *Math and the Mona Lisa: The Art and Science of Leonardo Da Vinci*. Smithsonian Books, 2004.

Barrett, Andrea. "The Sea of Information." *Best American Essays 2005*, edited by Susan Orlean, Houghton Mifflin, 2005, pp. 9–20.

Bassot, Barbara. *The Reflective Journal*. Palgrave Macmillan, 2013.

Berdan, Stacie Nevandomski, et al. *A Parent Guide to Study Abroad*. Institute of International Education, 2015.

———. *A Student Guide to Study Abroad*. Institute of International Education, 2013.

Birkenmaier, Anke, and Esther Whitfield, editors. *Havana beyond the Ruins: Cultural Mappings after 1989.* Duke UP, 2011.

"The Birth of the Eiffel Tower: A Realized Utopia." *Google Arts and Culture,* Google Cultural Institute, www.google.com/culturalinstitute/beta/exhibit/AQJMpLxJ. Accessed 8 Aug. 2016.

Block, David. *Second Language Identities.* Continuum, 2007.

Blumenfeld, P., et al. "Creating Usable Innovations in Systemic Reform: Scaling-up Technology-Embedded Project-Based Science in Urban Schools." *Educational Psychologist,* vol. 35, no. 3, 2002, pp. 149–64.

Braly, Jean-Philippe. "Paris, City of Maths." *CNRS International Magazine,* no. 13, April 2009, www2.cnrs.fr/en/1437.htm. Accessed 8 Aug. 2016.

Brecht, Richard, and A. Ronald Walton. "Policy Issues in Foreign Language and Study Abroad." *Annals of the American Academy of Political and Social Sciences,* vol. 532, 1994, pp. 213–25.

Brecht, Richard, et al. "Predicting and Measuring Language Gains in Study Abroad Settings." Freed, *Second Language Acquisition,* pp. 37–66.

Brown, Dan. *The Da Vinci Code.* Doubleday, 2003.

Brown, J. S., et al. "Situated Cognition and the Culture of Learning." *Educational Researcher,* vol. 18, no.1, 1989, pp. 32–41.

Brubaker, Cate. "Six Weeks in the Eiffel: A Case for Culture Learning during Short-Term Study Abroad." *Die Unterrichtspraxis / Teaching German,* vol. 40, no. 2, Fall 2007, pp. 118–23.

Buber, Martin. "I and Thou." Translated by W. Kaufmann. *The Continental Ethics Reader,* edited by M. Calarco and P. Atterton, Routledge, 2003.

Byrnes, Heidi, editor. *Learning Foreign and Second Languages: Perspectives in Research and Scholarship.* 2nd ed., Modern Language Association, 1998.

Camille Claudel. Directed by Bruno Nuytten, Gaumont, 1998.

Caravaggio. Directed by Derek Jarman, Cinevista, 1986.

Carlson, Jerry S., et al. *Study Abroad: The Experience of American Undergraduates.* Greenwood Press, 2015.

Carney, Terri M. "Reaching Beyond Borders through Service Learning." *Journal of Latinos and Education,* vol. 3, no. 4, 2004, pp. 267–71.

Chessman, Harriet Scott. *Lydia Cassatt Reading the Morning Paper.* Plume, 2002.

Chevalier, Tracy. *The Lady and the Unicorn: A Novel.* Dutton, 2004.

Chomsky, Noam. *Language and Mind.* 3rd ed., Cambridge University Press, 2006.

Christensen, Matthew B. *Decoding China: A Handbook for Traveling, Studying, and Working in Today's China.* Tuttle, 2013.

Cohen, A. D., et al. "Maximizing Study Abroad through Language and Culture Strategies: Research on Students, Study Abroad Program Professionals, and Language Instructors." *Final Report to the International Research and Studies Program, Office of International Education, DOE,* Center for Advanced Research on Language Acquisition, U of Minnesota, Minneapolis, 2005.

Collentine, Joseph, and Barbara F. Freed. "Learning Context and Its Effects on Second Language Acquisition." *Studies in Second Language Acquisition*, vol. 26, no. 2, 2004, pp. 153–71.

Common European Framework of Reference for Languages: Learning, Teaching, Assessment. Council of Europe, 2016, www.coe.int/t/dg4/linguistic/Source/ Framework_EN.pdf. Accessed 15 July 2016.

Conran, Mary. "They Really Love Me! Intimacy in Volunteer Tourism." *Annals of Tourism Research*, vol. 38, no. 4, Oct. 2011, pp. 1454–73, doi.org/10.1016/j .annals.2011.03.014.

"Courses: English." *2018–2019 Catalog*, University of Hawai'i Mānoa, www .catalog.hawaii.edu/courses/departments/eng.htm.

Cowell, Stephanie. *Claude and Camille*. Broadway Books, 2011.

Cummins, Jim. *Negotiating Identities: Education for Empowerment in a Diverse Society*. 2nd ed., California Association for Bilingual Education, 2001.

Dai, David Yun, and Robert J. Sternberg, editors. *Motivation, Emotion, and Cognition*. Lawrence Erlbaum Associates, 2004.

Deardorff, Darla K. "Intercultural Competence: A Definition, Model and Implications for Education Abroad." *Developing Intercultural Competence and Transformation: Theory, Research, and Application in International Education*, edited by Victor Savicki, Stylus Publishing, 2008, pp. 32–52.

Deardorff, Darla K., et al., editors. *The Sage Handbook of International Higher Education*. Sage, 2012.

Denhard, Rosanne Fleszar. "Engl 372/Engl 372H: Arts of Medieval and Renaissance Britain Travel Course." *MCLA: Massachusetts College of Liberal Arts in the Berkshires*, www.mcla.edu/Academics/undergraduate-experience/travel courses/england/index.

DePaul, Stephen C., and William W. Hoffa, editors. *A History of U.S. Study Abroad: Beginnings to 1965*. Special publication by *Frontiers: The Interdisciplinary Journal of Study Abroad* and The Forum on Education Abroad, 2010.

Dewey, John. *Experience and Education*. Simon and Schuster, 1997.

DeYoung, Paul, and Paul Primak. "The Education-Abroad Office in Its Campus Context." *NAFSA's Guide to Education Abroad for Advisers and Administrators*, edited by William Hoffa and John Pearson, NAFSA: Association of International Educators, 1997, pp. 17–26.

Doerr, Neriko M. "Study Abroad as 'Adventure': Globalist Construction of Host-Home Hierarchy and Governed Adventurer Subjects." *Critical Discourse Studies*, vol. 9, no. 3, 2012, pp. 257–68.

Dufon, Margaret A., and Eton E. Churchill, editors. *Language Learners in Study Abroad Contexts*. Multilingual Matters, 2006.

Duiker, K. Sello. *Thirteen Cents*. 2000. Ohio UP, 2013.

Dunn, William E., and James P. Lantolf. "Vygotsky's Zone of Proximal Development and Krashen's i+1: Incommensurable Constructs; Incommensurable Theories." *Language Learning*, vol. 48, 1998, pp. 411–42.

"Duration of Study Abroad." *Open Doors Report on International Exchange*, Institute of International Education, 2017, www.iie.org/Research-and-Insights/ Open-Doors/Data/US-Study-Abroad/Duration-of-Study-Abroad. Accessed 12 April, 2018.

Eaton, Charlie, et al. "Bankers in the Ivory Tower: The Financialization of Governance at the University of California." IRLE Working Paper No. 151-13, 2013, irle.berkeley.edu/files/2013/Bankers-in-the-Ivory-Tower.pdf.

Eaton, Charlie, et al. "The Financialization of US Higher Education." *Socioeconomic Review*, vol. 14, no. 3, 8 Feb. 2016, pp. 507–35, doi.org/10.1093/ser/ mwv030.

"Elegant Shape of the Eiffel Tower Solved Mathematically by CU-Boulder Prof." *CU Boulder Today*, U of Colorado, 5 Jan. 2005, www.colorado.edu/ today/2005/01/04/elegant-shape-eiffel-tower-solved-mathematically-cu -boulder-prof. Accessed 8 Aug. 2016.

Engberg, Mark, and T. J. Jourian. "Intercultural Wonderment and Study Abroad." *Frontiers: The Interdisciplinary Journal of Study Abroad*, vol. 25, Spring 2015, pp. 1–19, frontiersjournal.org/wp-content/uploads/2015/09/ ENGBERG-JOURIAN-FrontiersXXV-InterculturalWondermentandStudy Abroad.pdf. Accessed 18 July 2016.

Engestrom, Yrjo. "'Non Scholae sed Vitae Discimus': Toward Overcoming the Encapsulation of School Learning." *Learning and Instruction*, vol. 1, no. 3, 1991, pp. 243–59.

Espinoza, Maria. *Study Abroad in Spain: Everything You Need to Know About Studying in Spain*. CreateSpace Independent Publishing Platform, 2017.

"Essential Learning Outcomes." Association of American Colleges and Universities, 2008, www.aacu.org/leap/essential-learning-outcomes.

"Ethnomathematics and STEM Institute." *University of Hawai'i at Mānoa Ethnomathematics and STEM Institute*, ethnomath.coe.hawaii.edu/resources.php. Accessed 8 Aug. 2016.

Euclid. *Euclid's Elements*. Edited by Dana Densmore, translated by T. L. Heath, Green Lion Press, 2002.

Eyler, Janet, et al. *A Practitioner's Guide to Reflection in Service Learning*. Vanderbilt UP, 1996.

"Fields of Study." *Open Doors Report on International Exchange*, Institute of International Education, 2017, www.iie.org/Research-and-Insights/Open-Doors/ Data/US-Study-Abroad/Fields-of-Study. Accessed 12 April 2018.

Figes, Eva. *Light*. Plume, 2002.

Fornet, Ambrosio. *Narrar la nación: Ensayos en blanco y negro*. Editorial Letras Cubanas, 2009.

Fortus, David, et al. "Design-Based Science and Real-World Problem-Solving." *International Journal of Science Education*, vol. 27, 2005, pp. 855–79.

Freed, Barbara F. "An Overview of Issues and Research in Language Learning in a Study Abroad Setting." *Frontiers: The Interdisciplinary Journal of Study Abroad*, vol. 4, no. 2, 1998, pp. 31–60.

———, editor. *Second Language Acquisition in a Study Abroad Context.* John Benjamins, 1995.

Freed, Barbara F., et al. "Contexts of Learning and Second Language Fluency in French: Comparing Regular Classrooms, Study Abroad, and Intensive Domestic Programs." *Studies in Second Language Acquisition,* vol. 26, 2004, pp. 275–301.

"Freedom Park: Vision, Mission and Strategic Goals." *Freedom Park: A Heritage Destination,* An Agency of the Department of Arts and Culture, Republic of South Africa, www.freedompark.co.za/about-us/overview/vision-mission -and-strategic-goals.html. Accessed 25 Mar. 2016.

Freiberger, Marianne. "The Art Gallery Problem." *Plus Magazine,* 14 June 2014, plus.maths.org/content/art-gallery-problem?src=aop. Accessed 8 Aug. 2016.

Freire, Pablo. *Pedagogy of the Oppressed.* Translated by Myra Bergman Ramos, Continuum, 1970.

Friedman, Zack. "Student Loan Debt in 2017: A $1.3 Trillion Crisis." *Forbes,* 21 Feb. 2017, www.forbes.com/sites/zackfriedman/2017/02/21/student-loan -debt-statistics-2017/#f77fd165daba.

"Galileo Galilei." *History.com,* www.history.com/topics/galileo-galilei. Accessed 8 Aug. 2016.

Gándara, Patricia, and Francis Contreras. *The Latino Educational Crisis: The Consequences of Failed Social Policies.* Harvard UP, 2009.

García, Ofelia, and Clare E. Sylvan. "Pedagogies and Practices in Multilingual Classrooms: Singularities in Pluralities." *Modern Language Journal,* vol. 95, no. 3, Sept. 2011, pp. 385–400.

Gasta, Chad M. "Cross-Cultural Knowledge, Business Practices and Student Learning via Study Abroad." *Global Business Language,* vol. 13, 2008, pp. 29–44.

Gasta, Chad M., et al. "A Culture-Based Entrepreneurship Program: Impact on Student Interest in Business Ownership." *International Journal of Family Business,* vol. 4, 2007, pp. 17–30.

Gay, Geneva. *Culturally Responsive Teaching: Theory, Research, and Practice.* Teachers College Press, 2000.

Gerhard Richter. Directed by Corinna Belz, Zero One, 2012.

Ghyka, Matila. *The Geometry of Art and Life.* 2nd rev. ed., Dover, 1977.

Giedt, Todd, et al. "International Education in the 21st Century: The Importance of Faculty in Developing Study Abroad Research Opportunities." *Frontiers: The Interdisciplinary Journal of Study Abroad,* vol. 26, Fall 2015, pp. 167–86, frontiersjournal.org/wp-content/uploads/2015/11/GIEDT-GOK CEK-GHOSH-FrontiersXXVI-InternationalEducationinthe21st-Century.pdf. Accessed 27 July 2016.

Ginsburg, Ralph, and Laura Miller. "What Do They Do? Activities of Students during Study Abroad." *Language Policy and Pedagogy: Essays in Honor of A. Ronald Walton,* edited by R. Lambert and Elana Shohamy, John Benjamins, 2000, pp. 237–61.

Girl with a Pearl Earring. Directed by Peter Webber, Lions Gate, 2003.

Glye, Paul. "Study Abroad in a Time of Terror: U.S. Student Experiences in Brussels." *Frontiers: The Interdisciplinary Journal of Study Abroad*, vol. 29, no. 1, April 2017, pp. 15–27.

Gordimer, Nadine. *July's People.* Penguin, 1981.

Gore, Joan. *Dominant Beliefs and Alternative Voices: Discourse, Belief, and Gender in American Study Abroad.* Routledge, 2005.

Goya in Bordeaux. Directed by Carlos Saura, Andres Vincente Gomez, 1999.

Goya's Ghosts. Directed by Milos Forman, Samuel Goldwyn Films, 2007.

Guerra, Wendy. *Everyone Leaves.* Translated by Achy Obejas, Amazon Crossing, 2012. Translation of *Todos se van*, Bruguera, 2006.

Gutiérrez, Pedro Juan. *Dirty Havana Trilogy: A Novel in Stories.* Translated by Natasha Wimmer, Ecco, 1992.

Hamir, Heather Barclay, and Nick J. Gozik, editors. *Promoting Inclusion in Education Abroad: A Handbook of Research and Practice.* Stylus Publishing, 2018.

Hellebrandt, Josef, and Lucía T. Varona, editors. *Construyendo Puentas (Building Bridges): Concepts and Models for Service Learning in Spanish.* American Association for Higher Education, 1999.

Hoffa, William. *A History of U.S. Study Abroad: Beginnings to 1965.* Forum on Education Abroad, 2007.

Hoffa, William, et al., editors. *NAFSA's Guide to Education Abroad for Advisers and Administrators.* NAFSA: Association of International Educators, 1993.

Huebner, Thom. "The Effects of Overseas Language Programs: Report on a Case Study of an Intensive Japanese Course." Freed, *Second Language Acquisition*, pp. 171–93.

———. "Methodological Considerations in Data Collection for Language Learning in a Study Abroad Context." *Frontiers: The Interdisciplinary Journal of Study Abroad*, vol. 4, no. 1, 1998, pp. 1–30.

Hutchison, Yvette. *South African Performance and Archives of Memory.* Manchester UP, 2013.

IIE Passport 2014–15: The Complete Guide to Study Abroad Programs. Institute of International Education, 2014.

"IIE Releases Open Doors 2017 Data." Press release. Institute of International Education, 13 Nov. 2017, www.iie.org/Why-IIE/Announcements/2017-11-13 -Open-Doors-Data. Accessed 22 Mar. 2018.

Imagined Lives: Portraits of Unknown People. National Portrait Gallery, London, 15 Mar. 2012.

"Institute of International Education Leads Coalition to Double Number of Students Who Study Abroad by End of Decade." Press release. Institute of International Education, 3 Mar. 2014. www.iie.org/Why-IIE/Announcements/ 2014-03-03-Generation-Study-Abroad. Accessed 27 July 2016.

Jackson, Jane. *Language, Identity and Study Abroad: Sociocultural Perspectives.* Equinox, 2008.

Jochum, Christopher J. "Measuring the Effects of a Semester Abroad on Students' Oral Proficiency Gains: A Comparison of At-Home and Study Abroad." *Frontiers: The Interdisciplinary Journal of Study Abroad*, Fall 2014, pp. 93–104.

Joyce, David. "Euclid's Elements." Department of Mathematics and Computer Science, Clark U, 1996–98, mathcs.clarku.edu/~djoyce/java/elements/elements.html. Accessed 8 Aug. 2016.

Kibbe, Devin. "The 16th-Century 'Photograph': A Study of British Miniatures." *Metamorphosis*, Council of Public Liberal Arts Colleges (COPLAC), Fall 2010, metamorphosis.coplac.org/index.php/metamorphosis/issue/archive. Accessed 7 Aug. 2016.

Kinginger, Celeste. "Enhancing Language Learning in Study Abroad." *Annual Review of Applied Linguistics*, vol. 31, 2011, pp. 58–73.

———. *Language Learning and Study Abroad: A Critical Reading of Research*. Palgrave Macmillan, 2009.

———. "Language Learning in Study Abroad: Case Studies of Americans in France." *Modern Language Journal*, vol. 92, supp. 1, Dec. 2008, pp. 1–124.

Kinginger, Celeste, et al. "Contextualized Language Practices as Sites for Learning: Mealtime Talk in Short-Term Chinese Homestays." *Applied Linguistics*, vol. 37, no. 5, 2014, doi:10.1093/applin/amu061.

Kinginger, Celeste, et al. "The Short-Term Homestay as a Context for Language Learning: Three Case Studies of High School Students and Host Families." *Study Abroad Research in Second Language Acquisition and International Education*, vol. 1, 2016, pp. 34–60.

Klimt. Directed by Raul Ruiz, Film-Line Produktion, 2006.

The Knight of the Burning Pestle. By Francis Beaumont, directed by Adele Thomas, 12 Mar. 2014, Wanamaker Playhouse at Shakespeare's Globe Theatre, London.

Kozulin, Alex. *Psychological Tools: A Sociocultural Approach to Education*. Harvard UP, 1997.

Krajcik, Joseph S., et al. "Middle School Students' Initial Attempts at Inquiry in Project-Based Science Classrooms." *Journal of the Learning Sciences*, vol. 7, 1998, pp. 313–50.

Kramsch, Claire, editor. *Language Acquisition and Language Socialization: Ecological Perspectives*. Continuum, 2002.

Kuh, George D. "High-Impact Educational Practices: A Brief Overview." *High-Impact Educational Practices: What They Are, Who Has Access to Them, and Why They Matter*, Association of American Colleges and Universities, 2008, www.aacu.org/leap/hips. Accessed 7 Aug. 2016.

Lahiri, Jhumpa. *In Altre Parole*. Ugo Guanda, 2015.

———. "Teach Yourself Italian." *The New Yorker*, translated by Ann Goldstein, 7 Dec. 2015, www.newyorker.com/magazine/2015/12/07/teach-yourself-italian.

Lantis, Jeffrey S., and Jessica DuPlaga. *The Global Classroom: An Essential Guide to Study Abroad*. Paradigm, 2010.

Lantolf, James. "Sociocultural Theory: A Dialogic Approach to L2 Research." *Handbook of Second Language Acquisition*, edited by Susan Gass and Alison Mackey, Taylor and Francis, 2012, pp. 57–72.

Lantolf, James P., and Steven L. Thorne. *Sociocultural Theory and the Genesis of Second Language Development*. Oxford UP, 2006.

Lautréamont, Agathe. "Institut Henri Poincaré: Cédric Villani aura son musée des maths!" *Exponaute*, 16 Dec. 2015, www.exponaute.com/magazine/2015/12/16/institut-henri-poincare-cedric-villani-aura-son-musee-des-maths/. Accessed 8 Aug. 2016.

Lewin, Ross, editor. *The Handbook of Research and Practice in Study Abroad: Higher Education and the Quest for Global Citizenship*. Routledge, 2009.

Li Jin. "When in China, Do as the Chinese Do? Learning Compliment Responding in a Study Abroad Program." *Chinese as a Second Language Research*, vol. 1, no. 2, 2012, pp. 211–40.

Lier, Leo van. *The Ecology and Semiotics of Language Learning: A Sociocultural Perspective*. Kluwer Academic Publishers, 2004.

Liu Junru. *Chinese Food*. Cambridge UP, 2011.

Liu Li. "Language Proficiency, Reading Development, and Learning Context." *Frontiers: The Interdisciplinary Journal of Study Abroad*, Fall 2014, pp. 73–92.

Lodoli, Marco. *Isole; guida vagabonda di Roma*. Einaudi, 2005.

Looney, Dennis, and Natalia Lusin. *Enrollments in Languages Other Than English in United States Institutions of Higher Education, Summer 2015 and Fall 2016: Preliminary Report*. Modern Language Association, 2018, www.mla.org/content/download/83540/2197676/2016-Enrollments-Short-Report.pdf. Accessed 22 Mar. 2018.

Loveland, Elaina, and Christopher Murphy. "Leaders Speak Out." *International Educator*, vol. 15, 2006, pp. 30–35, www.nafsa.org/_/File/_/International Educator/EdAbroadJanFeb.pdf. Accessed 27 July 2016.

Lust for Life. Directed by Vincente Minnelli and George Cukor, MGM, 1956.

Mandela, Nelson. *Long Walk to Freedom: The Autobiography of Nelson Mandela*. 1995. Back Bay, 2013.

Mangen, Anne. "The Disappearing Trace and the Abstraction of Inscription in Digital Writing." *Exploring Technology for Writing and Writing Instruction*, edited by Kristine E. Pytash and Richard E. Ferdig, IGI Global, 2014, pp. 100–13.

Martínez, Ramón Antonio. "Spanglish as Literacy Tool: Toward an Understanding of the Potential Role of Spanish-English Code-Switching in the Development of Academic Literacy." *Research in the Teaching of English*, vol. 45, no. 2, 2010, pp. 124–49.

Martinsen, Rob. "Predicting Changes in Cultural Sensitivity among Students of Spanish during Short-Term Study Abroad." *Hispania*, vol. 94, no. 1, Mar. 2011, pp. 121–41.

Mayle, Peter. *Chasing Cezanne*. Vintage, 1998.

McKeown, Joshua S. *The First Time Effect: The Impact of Study Abroad on College Student Intellectual Development*. State U of New York P, 2009.

Mendelson, Vija G. "'Hindsight Is 20/20': Student Perceptions of Language Learning and the Study Abroad Experience." *Frontiers: The Interdisciplinary Journal of Study Abroad*, vol. 10, no. 3, 2004, pp. 43–63.

Miller-Perrin, Cindy, and Don Thompson. "The Development of Vocational Calling, Identity, and Faith in College Students: A Preliminary Study of the Impact of Study Abroad." *Frontiers: The Interdisciplinary Journal of Study Abroad*, vol. 19, Fall-Winter 2010, pp. 87–103, frontiersjournal.org/wp-content/uploads/2015/09/PERRINMILLER-THOMPSON-FrontiersXIX-The DevelopmentofVocationalCallingIdentityandFaithinCollegeStudents.pdf. Accessed 27 July 2016.

Mitchell, Rosamond, et al. "The Influence of Social Networks, Personality and Placement Types on Language Learning During Residence Abroad: Preliminary Findings of the LANGSNAP Project." Residence Abroad, Social Networks and Second Language Learning Conference, U of Southampton, 22 July 2013.

Morris, Frank A. "Serving the Community and Learning a Foreign Language: Evaluating a Service-Learning Programme." *Language, Culture and Curriculum*, vol. 14, no. 3, 2001, pp. 244–55.

Mr. Turner. Directed by Mike Leigh, Columbia, 2014.

Naturale, Joan Marie. *Seeing the World through Deaf Eyes: Chile Study-Abroad Experiences of Deaf Students*. 2014. St. John Fisher College, PhD dissertation, fisherpub.sjfc.edu/education_etd/213. Accessed 20 July 2016.

Nazario, Sonia. *Enrique's Journey*. Random House, 2006.

Ochs, Elinor. "Constructing Social Identity: A Language Socialization Perspective." *Intercultural Discourse and Communication: The Essential Readings*, edited by Scott F. Kiesling and Christina Bratt Paulston, Blackwell, 2005, pp. 78–91.

Paley, Vivian Gussin. *White Teacher*. Harvard UP, 2000.

Pasolini, Pier Paolo. "Profezia." *Tutte le poesie*, edited by Walter Siti, vol. 1, A. Mondadori, 2003.

———. *Ragazzi di vita*. 1955. Garzanti, 2014.

Paton, Alan. *Cry, the Beloved Country*. 1948. Scribner, 2003.

Patron, Marie-Claire. *Culture and Identity in Study Abroad Contexts: After Australia, French without France*. Peter Lang, 2007.

Pavlenko, Aneta. "New Approaches to Concepts in Bilingual Memory." *Bilingualism: Language and Cognition*, vol. 2, 1999, pp. 209–30.

Pavlenko, Aneta, and James P. Lantolf. "Second Language Learning as Participation and the (Re)construction of Selves." *Sociocultural Theory and Second Language Learning*, edited by James P. Lantolf, Oxford UP, 2000, pp. 155–77.

Pellegrino-Aveni, Valerie. *Study Abroad and Second Language Use: Constructing the Self*. Cambridge UP, 2005.

Perry, Lane, et al. "More Than a Vacation: Short-Term Study Abroad as a Critically Reflective, Transformative Learning Experience." *Creative Education*, vol. 3, no. 5, Sept. 2012, pp. 679–83, file.scirp.org/pdf/CE20120500014_92360488.pdf. Accessed 7 Aug. 2016.

Picasso and Braque Go to the Movies. Directed by Arne Glimcher, Arthouse Films, 2008.

Plann, Susan J. "Latinos and Literacy: An Upper-Division Spanish Course with Service Learning." *Hispania*, vol. 85, no. 2, 2002, pp. 330–38.

Poag, Trevor, and Jill Sperandio. "Changing Minds: The Impact of Study Abroad Components on Students' Changes in Their Religious Faith." *Frontiers: The Interdisciplinary Journal of Study Abroad*, vol. 26, Fall 2015, pp. 144–63, frontiersjournal.org/wp-content/uploads/2015/11/POAG -SPERANDIO-FrontiersXXVI-ChangingMinds.pdf. Accessed 27 July 2016.

The Rape of Europa. Directed by Richard Berge et al., Menemsha Films, 2006.

Rexeisen, Richard J., et al. "Study Abroad and Intercultural Development: A Longitudinal Study." *Frontiers: The Interdisciplinary Journal of Study Abroad*, vol. 17, Fall 2008, pp. 1–20, frontiersjournal.org/wp-content/uploads/2015/09/REXEISENetal-FrontiersXVII-StudyAbroadandIntercultural Development.pdf. Accessed 27 July 2016.

Ruiz, Richard. "Reorienting Language-as-Resource." *International Perspectives on Bilingual Education: Policy, Practice and Controversy*, edited by J. Petrovic, Information Age, 2010, pp. 155–72.

Russel, Dominic, et al. "The Financialization of Higher Education: What Swaps Cost Our Schools and Students." The Roosevelt Institute, 2016, p. 5, rooseveltinstitute.org/wp-content/uploads/2016/09/Financialization-of -Higher-Education.pdf. Accessed 11 May 2017.

Salisbury, Mark. "We're Muddying the Message on Study Abroad." *The Chronicle of Higher Education*, 30 July 2012, chronicle.com/article/Were-Muddying -the-Message-on/133211/.

Sandman, L. R., et al. "Center and Periphery in Service Learning and Community Engagement: A Postcolonial Approach." *Understanding Service Learning and Community Engagement: Crossing Boundaries through Research*, edited by Julie A. Hatcher and Robert G. Bringle, Information Age, 2012, pp. 25–46.

Savage, Baron L., and Haning Z. Hughes. "How Does Short-Term Foreign Language Immersion Stimulate Language Learning?" *Frontiers: The Interdisciplinary Journal of Study Abroad*, Fall 2014, pp. 104–20.

Savicki, Victor, and Elizabeth Brewer. *Assessing Study Abroad: Theory, Tools, and Practice.* Stylus Publishing, 2015.

Scribner, Sylvia. "Studying Working Intelligence." *Everyday Cognition: Its Development in Social Context*, edited by Barbara Rogoff and Jean Lave, Harvard UP, 1984, pp. 9–40.

Soneson, Heidi. "Education Abroad Advising to Students with Disabilities." NAFSA: Association of International Educators, 2009.

The Song of Songs. By Giovanni Pierluigi da Palestrina, conducted by Stephen Williams, performed by Chapter House Choir, 15 Mar. 2008, York Minster, York, UK.

Spenader, Allison, and Peggy Retka. "The Role of Pedagogical Variables in Intercultural Development: A Study of Faculty Development." *Frontiers: The Interdisciplinary Journal of Study Abroad*, vol. 25, Spring 2015, pp. 20–36, frontiersjournal.org/wp-content/uploads/2015/09/SPENADER-RETKA -FrontiersXXV-TheRoleofPedagogicalVariablesinInterculturalDevelopment. pdf. Accessed 27 July 2016.

Stein, Gertrude. *The Autobiography of Alice B. Toklas.* 1933. Vintage, 1990.

———. *Picasso.* 1938. Dover, 1984.

Stemler, Steven, et al. "Development and Validation of the Wesleyan Inter-cultural Competence Scale (WICS): A Tool for Measuring the Impact of Study Abroad Experiences." *Frontiers: The Interdisciplinary Journal of Study Abroad*, vol. 24, Fall 2014, pp. 25–47, frontiersjournal.org/wp -content/uploads/2015/09/STEMLER-IMADA-SORKIN-FrontiersXXIV -DevelopmentandValidationoftheWesleyanInterculturalCompetence ScaleWICS.pdf. Accessed 27 July 2016.

Stewart, Vivian. "Succeeding Globally: Transforming the Teaching Profession." *International Educator*, vol. 22, no. 3, May-June 2013, pp. 82–87. www.nafsa .org/_/File/_/ie_mayjun13_forum.pdf.

Stillwell, John. *Mathematics and Its History.* 3rd ed., Springer, 2010. Undergradu-ate Texts in Mathematics.

Stivale, Charles J., editor. *Modern French Literary Studies in the Classroom: Peda-gogical Strategies.* Revised ed., Modern Language Association, 2004.

Story, Shelley. *Prepare for Departure: A Guide to Making the Most of Your Study Abroad Experience.* CreateSpace Independent Publishing Platform, 2016.

Stubbs, Nancy. "Financial Aid." Hoffa et al., pp. 39–48.

"Students with Disabilities." *Open Doors Report on International Exchange*, Insti-tute of International Education, 2017, www.iie.org/Research-and-Insights/ Open-Doors/Data/US-Study-Abroad/Students-with-Disabilities. Accessed 12 Apr. 2017.

Swaffer, Janet, and Katherine Arens. *Remapping the Foreign Language Curricu-lum: An Approach through Multiple Literacies.* Modern Language Association, 2006.

Tacelosky, Kathleen. "Service Learning as a Way to Authenticate Dialogue." *Hispania*, vol. 91, no. 4, 2008, pp. 877–86.

Tan, Dali, and Celeste Kinginger. "Exploring the Potential of High School Homestays as Contexts for Local Engagement and Negotiation of Difference." *Social and Cultural Aspects of Language Learning in Study Abroad*, edited by Celeste Kinginger, John Benjamins, 2013, pp. 155–77.

The Tempest. By William Shakespeare, directed by Tyler Prendergast, Yorick Shakespeare Club of the Massachusetts College of Liberal Arts, 11–13 Apr. 2013, North Adams, Massachusetts.

Thomas, J. W. *A Review of Research on Project-Based Learning.* The Autodesk Foundation, Mar. 2000, www.bie.org/images/uploads/general/9d06758fd34 6969cb63653d00dca55c0.pdf. Accessed 6 Aug. 2016.

United States, Congress, House. United States Code. Title 42, section 12101, Office of the Law Revision Counsel, 26 July 1990, uscode.house.gov.

Vande Berg, Michael, et al., editors. *Student Learning Abroad: What Our Students Are Learning, What They're Not, and What We Can Do About It.* Stylus Publishing, 2012.

Vavrus, Michael. *Transforming the Multicultural Education of Teachers.* Teachers College Press, 2002.

Vreeland, Susan. *Luncheon of the Boating Party.* Viking, 2007.

Vygotsky, Lev. *Mind in Society.* Harvard UP, 1980.

Wagner, Kathryn. *Dancing with Degas.* Bantam, 2010.

Walonen, Michael K. "Applying Geocritical Theory to the Study Abroad Learning Experience." *Frontiers: The Interdisciplinary Journal of Study Abroad,* vol. 25, Spring 2015, pp. 37–46, frontiersjournal.org/wp-content/ uploads/2015/09/WALONEN-FrontiersXXV-ApplyingGeocriticalTheory totheStudyAbroadLearningExperience.pdf. Accessed 6 June 2016.

Wang, Wenxia, and Jiening Ruan. "Historical Overview of Chinese Language Education for Speakers of Other Languages in China and the United States." *Chinese Language Education in the United States,* edited by Ruan et al., Springer, 2016, pp. 1–28.

Ward, David. *A Poetics of Resistance: Narrative and the Writings of Pier Paolo Pasolini.* Fairleigh Dickinson UP, 1995.

Wertsch, James. *Voices of Collective Remembering.* Cambridge UP, 2002.

When Paris Was a Woman. Directed by Grete Schiller, 1996.

Woman in Gold. Directed by Simon Curtis, The Weinstein Company, 2015.

Woolf, Michael. "Another *Mishegas:* Global Citizenship." *Frontiers: The Interdisciplinary Journal of Study Abroad,* vol. 19, Fall-Winter 2010, pp. 47–60.

Zachmann, Gayle. "Overseas Engagements: The Presence and Futures of Study Abroad." Stivale, pp. 208–17.

INDEX